AGILE PROJECT MANAGEMENT

BEGINNER'S STEP-BY-STEP GUIDE TO LEARNING SCRUM

Andy Vickler

Table of Contents

Introduction 1

Chapter One: Why Scrum? 2

    The Case Against the Traditional Management System 3

    Why Scrum? 7

Chapter Two: Scrums Works Efficiently 11

    What Scrum Achieves... 11

    What Makes Scrum Great? 13

    Will Scrum Work?.. 14

Chapter Three: The Scrum Team 19

    Product Owner 20

    ScrumMaster 24

    The Development Team 25

Chapter Four: Scrum Artifacts 28

    Product Backlog... 29

    Sprint 30

    Execution Phase 31

    Daily Scrum... 32

    Done 33

    Sprint Review... 33

Sprint Retrospective 34

Chapter Five: Agile Principles.................................... 35

Agile Principle 1 35

Agile Principle 2 36

Agile Principle 3 37

Agile Principle 4 38

Agile Principle 5 38

Agile Principle 6 39

Agile Principle 7 39

Agile Principle 8 40

Agile Principle 9 40

Agile Principle 10 41

Agile Principle 11 41

Agile Principle 12 42

Agile Principles at Work... 42

Chapter Six: Product Backlog 51

These Are Properly Detailed 51

The Emergent.. 52

Estimation 52

Priorities.. 53

Product Backlog Grooming 53

When Will the Product Backlog Be Ready? 54

Chapter Seven: Scrum Master.................................. 56

Scrum Master's Roles 57

Responsibilities of the Scrum Master 60

Authority Processing.. 62

Solution Expert 62

Shield against Interference 63

Scrum Master Skills 67

**Chapter Eight: Scrum Master vs. Project Manager
vs. Product Owner** 70

Traditional Project Management 70

Enter Scrum 72

Project Manager in Scrum 73

Scrum Master vs. Project Manager 75

The Differences 76

Scrum Master vs. Product Owner 78

Chapter Nine: The Scrum Team 81

Scrum Roles vs. Job Titles 81

How to Build a Scrum Team 82

The Development Team 83

The Product Owner 84

The Development Team Structure 85

Development Team's Responsibilities 88

Chapter Ten: Work Estimation 90

Cost of Work 90

What to Measure 91

The Ideal Days 92

Planning Poker 92

Velocity 96

Velocity Range 96

Misuse of Velocity 99

Chapter Eleven: In-Depth Scrum **101**

    Component vs. Feature Teams 102

    Feature Team Production 103

    Multiple Teams 105

    Release Train 107

Chapter Twelve: Why Scrum Is the Best Option

For Developers **110**

    Development Team Is in Control 110

    Building Increments 110

    Focus and Teamwork 111

    Skillful Team 112

    Mutual Understanding on Completion of Increment 112

    Right Thing 112

Chapter Thirteen: Running Multiple Projects **113**

    Decoding Portfolio Management 113

    Inflow Strategies 120

    Outflow Strategy Creation 123

    Limiting WIP 124

    In-Process Items 125

    What Products to Produce? 127

Conclusion **129**

References **130**

Introduction

This book contains proven steps and strategies for agile project management method using Scrum. You will learn about the basic principles of the agile method, and I will explain why there is a dire need to use Scrum in managing your projects. What are the steps in the Scrum method, and why is the traditional Waterfall method about to lose traction in the corporate world?

I have dedicated a chapter on why Scrum is efficient. Each argument in the chapter is backed by scientific evidence. Then we will talk about the Scrum team that is the backbone of the method.

You will have a comprehensive overview of the Scrum artifacts. For example, I will explain some key artifacts like the execution phase, the sprint review, and the sprint retrospective. If you are a manager in a company and are assigned to implement Scrum in the organization, this book is for you. You will learn the technical jargon, the technical terms, the roles and responsibilities of different designations, and techniques to run multiple projects on Scrum.

Chapter One

Why Scrum?

Many organizations cling to a beaten method of conducting and managing their operations in a set line of actions. They receive requirements from the people who are at the higher end of the chain. They work hard day and night to complete the job their high-ups ask them to do. Once they get briefings on the plan, they start acting on it. They leave no stone unturned on making the plan a success in a given period. They occasionally meet their boss or client to confirm if they are going on track in the execution of the project. If all is good, they finish the task successfully, although they miss out on a couple of deadlines in rectifying where they went wrong.

The likelihood of failure in this management style is high and is likely to be on the project deadline. When a deadline has passed, nobody involved will be happy, given the amount of time and resources already spent on the project.

So common was this problem that a new system had to be designed to address it. The newly established system is known as Scrum.

Scrum is a project management system that cuts resources and time that an organization needs to wrap up a project in time.

The Case Against the Traditional Management System

The traditional method to manage projects is typically designed for the people to make sure that they fulfill all the business requirements to initiate designing something. After they have met all the requirements, they initiate working on a design or a plan. They start making the plan work and then also test the outcome of the result. After that, the client walks in and gives a nod to the launch of the project. The plan targets making sure that everyone performs his or her task well. They must ensure that all the things written on the Gantt chart are done before the next step. They must finish the agreed-upon tasks on the set deadline to kick off the testing process.

When the teams are done working on what they have to do, they can determine if they did well throughout the project. If what they did is satisfactory, they are applauded, and they move on to the next task. If not, the job is given back to them to rectify where they went wrong. This method of applying one plan after another to make the project a success is known as the Waterfall Method. Let's see how many steps project managers have to take to complete a project through the Waterfall Method.

Step 1: Analyzing Requirements

In the first step, you have to analyze the requirements of the project. If you are working on software development or any other form of project creation team, you will need to know the business angle of what you are creating. You have to define the problems that your project is aiming to solve. You have to delineate how people will react to your solutions. After you have defined all the requirements, you have the desired input you need to move on to the project's next step.

Step 2: Design

The second step of your project is the mixture of all the steps you need to take to satisfy the requirements you have earlier on determined to do. In the world of software development, this is where you define your hardware architecture and software architecture, data storage, and programming language, etc. This is the part where you determine how your project will benefit the end-user.

Step 3: Implementation

The third step of this management method focuses on the implementation of the plan you have already prepared. You start constructing what you have already designed. You try to meet the standards you have already made in the previous steps. At this point, the development team comes into action and sets up the things discussed in the first couple of steps.

Step 4: Test

The fourth step of the Waterfall Method is the testing process. Everything is ready. The quality assurance sector of the project springs into action at this stage. They ensure that the development team did not make any mistakes in the development or design of the project. At this point, people realize what is wrong with their plan or if everything is perfectly right. If something is wrong, the quality assurance team sends it back to the development team.

Step 5: Approval

When the project implementers are satisfied with the project, the client jumps into the scene and gives the nod to launching the project. The Waterfall method works as such that if something goes wrong at a particular stage, you have to go back to that stage and see what is wrong. Let's say you missed something in the implementation stage, but the project implementation managers think that everything was right. But something was wrong with the project's blueprint, and the managers will have to review the blueprint and make necessary changes. There will be revisions and implementations until managers get the desired result. So, naturally, the Waterfall method causes immense delays in the processes and puts you behind schedule.

Let us take a look at what possible issues arise when you stanchly follow the Waterfall method.

Waterfall Method Encourages Blind Following of Plans

In the traditional method of managing tasks, people tend to pay more attention to how things are going to happen in the right moment without being mindful of how things are going on and whether, in the end, they will fall into place. While proper planning is highly important, it is also of high importance that quality checkers and developers understand how things will shape up in the end for the end-user or the client. The people involved in the project must immediately see how a specific step in the fulfillment of the project falls apart before they take it to the testing stage. In this way, you can rectify it before the testing stage, saving more time. Sadly, this does not happen in the Waterfall method.

High Consumption of Resources

Gliding back to the previous stage in the Waterfall method means that the money and time you have spent on the project will go down the drain because it will not produce any valuable product. This alludes to the fact that the management can waste all of its resources when it finds out that something fails to work at a particular stage. Then it naturally inclines toward spending more resources on going back to the previous stage and finding out what went wrong that produced unlikely results.

End-User Has No Clue of What Product They Get At the End

When the final stage of the project comes, and it is time to show the end-user your produce, the stakes are high that the end-user does not like the turnout of your product even though they demanded something else at the first stage of project development. It is quite easy for the end-user to change their preferences or quality requirements over time. The Waterfall system does not address this problem. You will have to revise your plans and redo your project to suit the client's changing needs.

Testing May Suffer

It is also possible that you start predicting accurate outcomes of the project without actually testing the project because of a lack of time. This results in unexpected results that damage the flow and quality of the project.

You Are Unaware of Which Stage You Are On

Since the product you are about to create is not going to be produced until you reach the final stage of the project, you are unsure if you are in the planning or developing stage of the project.

Waterfall is sometimes too risky since it is rigid and does not allow flexibility at any stage of development. If you have to produce a perfect product at the end of the day, you need a more flexible approach so that you don't have to get back to the drawing board when you present your product to the client and get rejected.

Why Scrum?

Scrum is one of the most popular agile methods and, there is something special behind the immense success of this method. The direct answer to what made Scrum so successful is that it is simple to use, straightforward to operate, and easily implemented. Although there are many iterative and incremental development methodologies like Agile Unified Process, Scrum is simpler than all of them. Its inherent characteristics make it simple. It is highly popular among project managers because it has very well-documented use cases.

Some Scrum users claim that the certifications helped Scrum become so much popular. Product owners, masters, and developers can get easily certified by Scrum Alliance.

Scrum is highly productive, and there are reasons behind that. The biggest reason behind its productivity is its mature framework of project management and development. With frequent and continuous iterations and feedback, it helps project managers make sure that the product is produced as per the customer's needs. The ability to change requirements ensures that the project does not derail during the development process.

Scrum offers immensely good processes, and it comes with brilliantly psychological benefits. It builds on several psychological mechanisms and some kind of smart motivation to help the teams boost their performance in developing the project.

Scrum aims at solving problems in the creation of a product by offering top-level flexibility. The framework helps you address complex and adaptive problems with a top productive value without compromising your productivity in the process. Scrum is generally based on the assumption that knowledge flows from what you have experienced already. It means that you only have the power to make decisions on things that are in your knowledge already. Since it works on existing knowledge, it usually implements an iterative and incremental approach to ensure that you have a good handle over all the risk factors involved in the process. You can also optimize the predictability of all the tasks in the project development phase. Here are the basic three pillars of Scrum.

Scrum Offers Transparency

The first pillar of Scrum is its high level of transparency. When you are working with Scrum, all the processes and steps and aspects are transparent to everyone responsible for bringing about the project outcomes. This means that everyone involved in the process knows when a certain part of the process is successful or completed in time. Also, everyone understands what steps need to be taken to ensure that the task is completed well in time and as per the aspirations.

Inspection

The second pillar of Scrum is inspection. Those involved in the development and implementation of a project have to check the progress and the facts when they are using Scrum. This helps them detect any variances that they do not want to include in the project. Everyone involved in the process knows that keeping a tab on your progress must not be involved in the way of the work.

Adaption

The third pillar of Scrum is adaption. Let's say the person who is inspecting the project and its progress sees that certain aspects of project management make the end product unacceptable. In that case, the materials and processes are adjusted immediately to bring about the desired outcome. These adjustments are usually made to cut down on the possible deviations of the result.

As Scrum tends to stand firm on these three pillars, people who use this framework do not feel the need to rely on only one team to fulfill the stages before they get an idea of what they have to create and if the product they are going to produce will work in the real world.

Scrum aims to eliminate the waiting period between the stages of development and implementation and points out what processes people will take care of. That makes it easy to understand if the people involved in the development will need any kind of corrections. This cuts down the time and budget that people ought to spend on the completion of projects.

Chapter Two

Scrums Works Efficiently

Scrum is a simple and lightweight system to manage heavy projects easily and efficiently. Its efficiency is apparent because big companies like Canon, Fuji-Xerox, and Honda have adopted the method to produce high quality and fast results. With the help of this framework, you can learn how you can create high-end projects through a brilliant project development system by using a scalable and team-based approach. While Scrum was popular as a system to develop software, its name was taken from the rugby sport. In the game, you have to restart the game when the ball shoots out of the play or someone accidentally commits any kind of infringement. Scrum, as a framework, tends to serve a similar purpose for project managers. Instead of keeping the game running despite a possible error, you have the opportunity to fix the error first and then play the game so that the chances of error in the result are minimum.

What Scrum Achieves

Scrum is an agile project management method. Therefore, you have to fulfill the backlog of a product. It consists of different features and capabilities that you must create to come up with a perfect product. The backlog will tell you the things that you must do at the start. If you run out of a resource to produce the product, any incomplete backlog item will exhibit a low level of priority than that of the completed work. Any project that is done by using Scrum is usually done in the form of short iterations. These iterations are called sprints, and they exist within time boxes, which range from a week to a calendar month. Throughout these iterations, a cross-functional team performs all the work.

The jobs include designing, building, and planning. You may include in them testing the product as well. After you have done the task, you will connect with the project stakeholders to get their feedback. The feedback of the project stakeholders will tell how many and what type of alterations are possible to make the perfect product. Once the feedback is processed toward the team, the team will plan how to deal with the next iteration.

If the stakeholder feedback mentions that the team has completed an episode of the project and they realize that there is a need for a new feature that the project team has not considered earlier on, the owner of the product can approve to include a new feature to the product in the backlog. Once it is included in it, the team can work on it in the next iteration. That's how the product keeps on improving.

As an iteration or sprint ends, the team produces a product that they can already launch, or they can also inject an addition to an existing product. If everyone has already decided that they will not be able to release the product after a finished iteration, everyone can decide to release features from more than one iteration.

What Makes Scrum Great?

Scrum is great because it offers a lot of benefits to project managers. Here is a rundown of what makes Scrum a great agile project management method and why you should not delay adopting it to complete your projects quickly.

High Customer Satisfaction

Scrum cuts down on the danger of missing deadlines that your customers set. It fully eliminates the danger of missing any customer needs. Instead of focusing on the features, Scrum looks forward to identifying what type of product will be useful to your end-user. When you have a clear view of the demands of your clients, you can envision the end product well. With a clear foresight of the end product, Scrum minimizes your risk of getting rejected by the client.

Minimum Resources

Scrum makes it possible that teams start working on the project as soon as they get a list of what they must accomplish. Instead of working on a plan that you must not break at any cost, Scrum demands that teams focus on wrapping up the backlogs created ahead of time. Since these plans are flexible, teams do not have to spend extra time on planning. Instead of that, valuable time and resources may be spent on building the product and maintaining the product.

Speed

Speed is another factor that makes Scrum the apple of every developer's eyes. Since people, who are using Scrum as a project management method, stay laser-focused on doing a working product than on creating the project architecture, this framework is likely to produce a top-quality product in less time.

More ROI

Organizations and clients who look forward to creating projects are more likely to enjoy an improved return on investment since the products created through Scrum are heavily tested to check their quality. Also, these products are launched earlier as well. Scrum enables developing teams to release more frequent improvements and smaller improvements from time to time to a product that has already been released, which appeals to stakeholders. In this way, all the stakeholders get better returns on investment.

Employ Satisfaction

Since the employees can measure their success and know that they contribute to a project's success, they feel motivated and are more engaged in developing projects. A higher motivational level of employees results in a better product when they go through iterations.

Will Scrum Work?

Scrum is an effective framework for several projects, but you should not consider it as a solution for all types of projects. It may offer an excellent solution in your organization, but it may not cater to the needs of a different organization. Realistically speaking, it does not have all the solutions for all the project types. The best thing is that you can check whether Scrum will work for your project or not. You can use the software known as Cynefin to make proper sense of the situations you may encounter throughout your project scenarios. There are some possible disorder scenario domains for you to find out whether Scrum will work or not.

Simple Scenarios

The scenarios that are considered simple are the situations in which everyone can clearly see the causes and effects. People know the right answer. This kind of domain is the best for repeatedly reproducing products since you can repeat some steps to solve some existing problems. While Scrum may be a way to address a certain type of scenario domain, you may achieve fast and certain results with the assembly line system since you already have legitimate practices anywhere.

Complicated Scenarios

Experts more often dominate the scenarios that are complicated to ensure good practices exist in a certain project. While the possibility of having multiple answers exist, having the services of an expert to detect problems would be efficient in addressing the right scenarios with multiple outcomes. Scrum can be used for the resolutions of these kinds of scenarios, but it is also a fact that Scrum may not be the best solution to deal with this kind of scenario.

Chaotic Scenario

These types of scenarios demand a solution. When your particular project enters the chaotic domain, you will experience a crisis that you need to handle and neutralize before it does any kind of additional harm and bring the situation back to the normal order. This is the kind of scenario you may experience when a person files a suit or does not find an expert.

Scrum is perfect for addressing different kinds of scenarios since you lack the luxury to prioritize backlogs and what you must do when another similar situation strikes. When you enter a chaotic situation, you must have someone who has full authority to take charge and act as well.

Disordered Scenario

A disordered scenario happens when you are uncertain of what stage you are working on in the project you are working on and do not know if your plans are working. This is a highly dangerous situation that you must break free from whenever you encounter. This demands that you break this situation apart and look at the disjointed components to know if they fall into any other category. When you find out the right category of these components, you can decide upon the approach you need to take to solve a situation and return to the development progress. You cannot adopt Scrum in this kind of situation until you categorize what components exist in a certain problem.

Interruption Scenarios

When you have a project that will experience multiple interruptions, you will not be able to use Scrum as a method. Take a different route to solve your problem in a scenario that suffers multiple interruptions. These scenarios will fill up your backlog faster, and you will not have the opportunity to work on them in the future.

Also, your backlog will frequently change, which makes iterations unreliable since you have little knowledge of what future iterations you need to do. You may receive top-priority backlogs that will keep you from achieving and planning the next iteration that you have in mind.

Workflows that have many interruptions demand an agile approach. Therefore, you may need to use an agile framework like Kanban to limit your work in the process. This will allow you to optimize the workflow, calculate how much progress you have made up until now, and see how you can improve your approach.

Complex Scenario

The complex degree problems make you realize that more unpredictable results exist than what you may expect from your approaches. In this particular domain, you are highly likely to have the right answer when correcting the hindsight and mistake. This demands you to explore the problem and inspect it to determine whether it is working or not. After that, you can adapt based on your knowledge that you have just gained from the exploration and inspection. This is also the same domain that you are likely to encounter when trying to make certain innovations or make enhancements for past projects that demand better features.

This is where Scrum truly shines since complex scenarios use your ability to initiate a probe in the situation and then inspect what you are likely to do in a specific timeframe. When you learn a better method in the iteration process, you may adapt it on the next iteration.

Chapter Three

The Scrum Team

Scrum is not something that you may label as a standard. You cannot follow it faithfully to make a guaranteed product that makes your customers happy. Also, you cannot use Scrum solely to develop any type of product within your budget and deadline. Instead, it is always a better approach to understand what Scrum is as a framework that enables you to manage and organize work in a better way. You may think of Scrum as a root of a tree. You cannot disregard a pattern or introduce changes to practice and principle without risking the tree's death. When working with Scrum, you can add the desired fixtures and customize the tree until you know the process and product that seem to work best for you.

It is crucial to keep the Scrum framework working to stick to the roles you assign to people. Each person who enters the Scrum management system is assigned a role, which he or she must keep playing until asked otherwise. Making Scrum work means that the people in the Scrum team can efficiently fulfill their roles to prevent possible problems from popping up along the way.

Product Owner

The first role we must discuss is the role of the owner of the product. The product owner is responsible for telling what needs to be developed. He also sets the order of the items that must be fulfilled throughout the action. You may consider him the single authority that tells the team what they must work on and create and what features they must integrate into the product. He is the one who tells other team members what they have to come up with.

For this reason, he must create the product backlog that contains the product goals that the development team must accomplish when they start working. The product owner ought to stay available all time so that when the development team and the ScrumMaster need to ask any question about the end product, they get their answer without wasting any time. The question may also relate to the product owner's goals in the backlog of the product. That's why the onus is on the product owner to make the product a success during the maintenance and development phase. The role of the product owner demands the fulfillment of the following tasks.

Management of Economics

There are many things that a product owner has to do to make sure that he manages the resources well when the team gets ready to start the development of the product. When he manages economics, he has to make sure that he is also managing the following.

The first section of economics management comes at the release level. At this particular point, the product owner needs to take a series of actions regarding the scope, date, quality, and budget. He receives information during the development stage of the product. If the product owner sees that the team produces a product that creates extra revenue if they work on an additional week, he must enter a trade-off for budget and final release of the product.

Also, he may opt to stop funding the additional week of work if the work planned to be done in the same timeframe does not mean creating an improved product. He may also decide that the team's goals should work on ought to change or that the team must stop the production phase because of the ever popping up problems encountered with all the other stakeholders.

The second stage of economics is sprint-level economics. It is the product owner's job to ensure a better return on investment (ROI) happening in each sprint occurring during the development of the product. Whenever they do economics at this certain level, they treat money that organization is using as if it belongs to them. This certainly makes them consider if the features they have to spend on are worth development.

The third stage is economics in the product backlog. The product owner is the one who has to create the backlog of the product. Therefore, he needs to introduce changes in the priorities in the list when any kind of economic change happens. For example, let's say your development team says that it needs to work more on a particular feature that was predicted earlier to take a modest amount of effort. He then sees all the benefits that everyone gets from this particular feature have changed. This prompts him to put a particular feature as a priority in exchange for a bigger task.

Planning Phase

During the product-planning phase, the product owner deals with the stakeholders to seek help to envision the product. When a sprint is properly accomplished, the product owner jumps back to stakeholders and other teams for defining what he has to do and accomplish next. When he is about to plan the sprint with the team, he actually gives his input that the team ought to look at what type of items in the backlog may be realistically completed in the timeframe of the sprint.

Backlog Creation

When the product owner grooms the backlog of the product, he takes great care of refining, estimation, and prioritizing or items that have been listed, not without the help of the Scrum team members. While the product owner may not have full knowledge of the process of development, he remains available for clarification and consultation when the development team foresees that amendments ought to be introduced to meet up the deadlines. This will ensure that your goals are updated as per the work you do during production and that the product backlog items keep flowing smoothly in the next sprints.

Building Criteria

The product owner must ensure that the goals that have been set and ought to be met in a sprint session are accomplished. He needs to make sure that the team meets the functional and non-functional requirements. He may consult with the experts to seek assistance from the development team. The criteria for acceptance are crucial to the Scrum team because it educates everyone on the project's progress. Without it, the development team will be unable to understand what defines a finished task. The team will also be unable to include standard practices while working on the next sprint.

Collaboration with the Development Team

The basic job of the product owner is a role that he must play every day since he has to stay engaged in different tasks of the development team to prevent delays on the essential feedback that may already be incorporated in a single day. It makes it possible for the product owner to see some specific features that have been initially required but that may no longer be required when other features have been done. When the product owner stays within reach and is ready to offer feedback, the organization tends to prevent unwanted expenses by establishing timely adaptations for best practices.

Working with Stakeholders

The product owner is the only voice of stakeholders that directly speaks to all the people involved in the production process. When the product owner can work closely with the persons involved in creating the product that is not part of the Scrum team, he could gather the input that he must have to create a coherent vision in the development. In this way, the Scrum team can prevent any emerging unwanted risks in the features that are contrary to the satisfaction of the customer and client.

ScrumMaster

Another role in Scrum is the role of ScrumMaster. A ScrumMaster takes care of team guidance in the development of the product. He is the one who makes people understand the basic principles, practices, and values that everybody needs to stick to, to achieve the success of a particular project. A Scrum Master usually serves as a coach that optimizes the performance by providing necessary and crucial leadership.

ScrumMaster helps in the resolution of any potential issues that arise from time to time. He also plays a role in making improvements on the projects. He ensures that the team remains protected from outside interferences and it removes things that hamper productivity. But ScrumMaster does not have complete control over the team. He tends to act as a leader and not as a traditional project manager.

As the main task of the Scrum Master is serving the coach, there needs to be a point in day-to-day activities when ScrumMaster does not have to guide the development team when the Scrum team accomplishes multiple sprints. Scrum is inherently designed to prevent different variances and instill efficiency in the work that is in progress in the organization. That's why the development team arrives at a point when it no longer needs coaching anymore. The ScrumMaster is highly relevant and valuable whenever the team wants to initiate a new sprint, and the team must incorporate a product backlog that has not been encountered before.

The Development Team

The development team of Scrum determines how to deliver the product owner's exact requirements. The team comprises different people who have different job descriptions, like a tester, a designer, an architect, and a database administrator. This allows them to cross-function. This also allows them to be dynamic when testing, designing and building a product that the product owner has requested. The development team has the most important job to do. That's why the team must have the capability to work in a self-organized manner to decide on the best way to meet all the goals that the product owner has already set. In the Scrum framework, the development team has the following key responsibilities to play.

Sprint Execution

Whenever a sprint happens, the members of the development team design, build, integrate, and test the items in the product backlog. They can do this by working in increments and producing potentially shippable features. The development team should be well-organized, self-organized, and collaborate to make decisions when managing, communicating, planning, and carrying out the work. They should spend the majority of their time on the execution of sprints.

Backlog Grooming

The second task that the development team ought to do is backlog grooming. Whenever some sprint happens or before the team kicks off the production of features, the development team tends to allot appropriate time to support the product owner when the task at hand is refining, prioritizing certain items, and creating some items on the backlog of the product.

Sprint Planning

The development team works with the ScrumMaster and product owner to develop certain goals to achieve over the next sprint. The development team has a greater responsibility of finding out which subset of the backlog of the product needs to be prioritized to attain the goals they have already been located.

Inspection and Adaptation

Whenever a sprint concludes, the development team starts reviewing product features they have accomplished through the previous sprints. They also review how many and what type of process and technical practices they have to adapt for their next sprints. Due to all these responsibilities, the development team has to stay sharp, self-sufficient, and highly capable of the cross-functionalities they have to counter. This means that the team must consist of people from a wide range of backgrounds. All these processes equip them with different types of cognitive skills. While all the development team members possess different kinds of specialties, they should adapt as individuals to the core discipline tasks. The development team usually has a set number of people. The right size is important. Scrum says that it is ideal that the development team is small and ranges between five and nine members. This size is crucial for the maintenance of high efficiency. If you keep the development team small, the chances are low that any member of the development team slacks around. In a bigger team, the development team members think that there is someone taking care of the work for them.

When the development team is small, you will have to spend less time communicating with them. In this way, constructive interaction is usually promoted inside a certain group with the help of a small team. Every team member realizes the importance of everyone else in the team, keeping harmful specialization at bay.

Managers and QA

Scrum does not need a large number of managers to make the entire team sustainable. They need to make sure that the ScrumMaster and the product owner need to work together to ensure that the development does the work that it needs to do. Some organizations attempt to implement separate installation and testing and recruit a QA team during the adaptation of the Scrum framework. The testing process is interwoven with the work that happens in all sprints. This is why the development team tests all finished features while still working on the ones yet to be accomplished.

Chapter Four

Scrum Artifacts

When an organization starts adhering to the Scrum framework, everyone in the development team and the stakeholders ought to make sure that the tasks at hand are properly completed. To measure how many tasks they have completed, they follow standard protocols that allow them to keep track of all the artifacts and activities they must accomplish. While Scrum makes it a point that the workflow in a given project is highly dynamic, it needs to follow a set of events. By adhering to the flow, people will determine what type of tasks they are presently doing and what achievements they need to make while producing the product. The flow of activities shows when they must adapt a better practice, when they have to do away with a feature, and when they must launch the product and let the end users review it. Take a look at the following artifacts and activities that each development team member must take care of creating the product or complete the product.

Product Backlog

This is the list that generally contains the things you need to accomplish in a project or a product. To obtain the list, the product owner, with aid from the Scrum Team and the stakeholders, creates a specific sequence of different tasks arranged as per their importance in the development of the product. The product backlog usually contains the initial version of the product master before a certain type of work is done. After a few iterations, it may contain different types of changes to change features that do not work out for them, that require repairs for them, and that need some improvements.

Some of the Scrum team members refer to the product backlog as the user story as this reminds them that they should either build or finish products to fulfill the end user's needs. During the process of the creation of stories and items, the product owner needs to define the following:

1. Who are the end-users? What type of users will be benefiting from the product?

2. What do you need to build?

3. What is the reason behind the importance of product features?

4. How much work a certain item needs before it is implemented?

5. What is the standard that tells you that the development team has properly correctly implemented the item?

Before you finalize everything, you have to look at the size of different items that find their place in the backlog. If the item in the product backlog is gigantic, it entails a greater cost. In different projects, the cost of the product must be determined to tell if it ought to be a priority for you. This is why many team members are inclined to use a term dubbed as a relative size measure. Using this specific measure, you can tell that the overall size of different items in the product backlog. Also, you can compare them with the size of different other items.

Sprint

The sprint in Scrum is an iteration that generally exists inside a particular timeframe. Within these sprints, the development team aims to create valuable things for the end-user. A backlog in a sprint serves as a to-do list that must be done within a particular duration. Within a sprint timeframe, the Scrum Master makes it a proper point that there will not be any reason for the development team to not meet some items in the backlog of a sprint. To achieve this, it is usually standard practice to ensure that no alteration is found in the previously expressed goals. There will be no changes in the backlog of a sprint, and there will be no changes in the number of personnel involved in a project. That's why it is standard practice that the ScrumMaster and the product owner agree on what should be included in the backlog of sprints. After that, the development team reviews what type of high-priority items can be achieved while the team does its job at a sustainable pace.

This alludes to the fact the development team usually has a say in what level of pace it should work on achieving what should be said in the backlog. To determine the right amount of pace, the development team has to divide the items that the ScrumMaster and the product owner agreed to do on a particular sprint into some smaller tasks. These tasks, later on, turn into items of that sprint backlog.

When the development team plans the sprint backlog, they formulate a coherent and comprehensive plan. They define how many hours they are going to need to accomplish the task. Since each sprint is supposed to force the development team to do tasks fast, the development team does not need much time for the planning phase. The sprint plan for one month is supposed to complete within eight hours. The development team ought to see if their tasks will fit inside the spring timeframe the ScrumMaster gives them. If it happens, they should repeat the work and check if more tasks need to be accommodated or not.

Execution Phase

When the Scrum development team completes the planning phase, and everyone gets the tasks they must accomplish over the next sprint, the development team starts working as per the guidelines issued by the ScrumMaster. The development team would only label the task as finished if they feel confident that all the crucial tasks for creating quality features have been accomplished. During this phase, nobody instructs the development team on what they have to do to achieve the specified items in the sprint backlog. Instead of staying directly managed, the development team tends to organize itself as per what makes them finish their tasks efficiently.

Daily Scrum

The development team members hold meetings over a day for inspecting their particular methods and see if any better practice exists by which they can adapt to improve their product quality, which they have accomplished in a particular sprint. This happens as a 15-minute huddle in the development team. The ScrumMaster aids them during the huddle. He does that by asking them the following key questions.

1. What has the development team accomplished since the latest daily Scrum?

2. What are the plans of the development team for the next Scrum?

3. What type of obstacles the development team may face is likely to prevent them from making further progress?

The team members have to answer these questions justly so that they can address the issues properly. When the team members have addressed them, they are better positioned to become highly aware of a bigger picture. They see if they are making progress or any modifications must be made in their activities.

Done

Everyone playing a role to accomplish a task must work on the concept of 'done.' They should understand the concept and agree to it before they jump to the other items in the product backlog that they agreed to resolve over the next sprint they encounter. When everyone agrees on this concept, they should reach the confidence that the amount of work they have already completed is of good quality and can be immediately shipped to the end-users.

When you imagine the concept of a shippable product, it should not be the product that the development team would deploy to the customers or the clients. When you are working in Scrum, the product, when prepared, is readily shippable to the end-user. However, shippable status for a product is only achieved when everyone is fully aware that the total amount of work accomplished is completely satisfactory and that no feature or work has been neglected throughout product development. This eventually means that the work accomplished is sufficient for the generation of feedback, determining if you have to add any extra features in the product backlog or if the product is ready to launch.

Sprint Review

When the development team accomplishes a sprint, the team members must inspect and adapt their product that everyone builds. The Scrum team, the customers, the sponsors, the stakeholders, and all the interested parties hold a full-fledged conversation to review different features. If a sprint is successfully reviewed, everyone who is not in the development team contributes ideas on developing and improving the process. This gives a broadened view of how the work is going and how it will affect the final product. This is where the customers, the stakeholders, the sponsors, and concerned parties pitch into the development direction.

Sprint Retrospective

Whenever the Scrum team receives feedback and review from others, they will kick off their own inspection and adaptation process. This is where everyone in the development team will discuss what worked for them and what they ought to slice off the processes. Once they are out of this phase, they are perfectly ready to plan how their next sprint will look based on assessing their technical processes and past workflow.

Chapter Five

Agile Principles

Twelve agile principles have been given and explained in The Agile Manifesto. These principles are aimed at agile software development, and they help establish tenets of the agile mindset. They are usually not rules for practicing agile methods but are a handful of principles to instill agile thinking.

Agile Principle 1

The first principle is setting up the highest priority to satisfy the customers through continuous and early delivery of software. The best ways for ensuring that the customers are happy while delivering valuable software are to ship earlier, iterate frequently, and then listen to the market continuously. Unlike the traditional approaches to developing the product, which has long cycles of development, agile principles encourage cutting down on time between ideation and a launch. The basic idea behind this is to put a working product into customers' hands at an earlier point. When you successfully do this, the product managers can quickly get a minimum viable product (MVP) into the world and then use it to get customer feedback. This particular feedback is fed and processed into the product's development process and is systematically used to produce better products through an informed production method.

What happens is that the product development teams use a minimum of viable products. They also use fast experimentation processes to validate ideas and test hypotheses. Different frequent releases help in fueling a regular feedback cycle between the product and the customer. You should not consider shipped and done the same thing. They are inherently different in Scrum. Instead of releasing a final product, iterations continue to improve the products based on market feedback and customer feedback.

Agile Principle 2

This principle deals with welcoming the requirements that frequently change even in the late stages of development. The agile processes tend to harness the change to ensure a competitive advantage for the customer. Change is considered a constant in this world. Agile values and principles support response to the changes rather than moving on despite seeing them. The previous approaches to developing the product are often averse to change, details, and documentation plans. But Scrum is change and detail-oriented, and it thrives on change. Agile principles support the observation of changing markets, competitive threats, customer needs, and changing course when it is necessary.

When you put this principle into practice, the product teams are usually guided by high-level strategic goals and even the themes below these goals. The product department's success is usually measured against the progress made toward the strategic goals rather than by delivering pre-defined feature sets. The product strategy and all the tactical plans are properly reviewed, shared, and adjusted regularly to reflect the changes and the new findings. Products need to appropriately manage the expectations of all the executive stakeholders and ensure that they understand why a certain change occurs.

Agile Principle 3

The third agile principle focuses on delivering working software more often within two weeks to two months. Of course, the preference is for a shorter timescale than a longer timescale. The agile philosophy favors breaking the development of a product into smaller components and then shipping more often. The agile approach reduces drafting time with the help of short-term development cycles of the smaller portions of your product. This is contrary to the traditional Waterfall method that consumes too much time, and demands big amounts of documentation. The most important thing is that the frequent-release approach tends to create a high level of opportunity for your teams to validate the product ideas and multiple strategies.

Agile product development cycles are often sprints and iterations that are broken down into product initiatives, ought to be completed within a set timeframe. More often, the timeframe spans between 2 and 4 weeks. Another alternative to agile sprints is a gradual but continuous development of products. The method of shipping software works less in terms of time boxes and works more in terms of deciding what should be done.

Agile Principle 4

The developers and business people ought to work together throughout your project. Communication is considered a critical component of the success of any team. The agile manifesto says that it takes a village to raise one child and that also applies to a product. A successful product needs insight from a particular organization's technical and business sides, which only happens if two teams work together. Regular communication between the developers and business people helps in improving alignment across an organization by building transparency and trust.

Agile Principle 5

The fifth agile principle revolves around building different projects around motivated individuals. You need to give them the support and environment they need and trust them to complete the job. One key part of agile philosophy is the empowerment of individuals and teams through autonomy and trust-building practices. The agile teams should be carefully built so that only the right people are included in the team with the right skill-sets to finish the job. Once you have selected the right people for the team, you should clearly define what responsibilities they have to fulfill before the project starts. Once you start the work, the agile method does not give room to hand-holding or micromanagement.

The product must ensure that engineering understands the requirements and strategy before the start of the development, which means that you will have to share users' stories and see the bigger picture that is properly outlined in the roadmap of the product.

Agile Principle 6

The sixth agile principle is about using the most effective and efficient method of information transmission within the development team. The method is a face-to-face conversation among team members. With many remote development teams, the principle receives a bit of critique. Effective communication with the development team is about jumping out of Slack and email and having face-to-face interactions. The main objective behind the principle is about encouraging the developers and people to communicate in real-time about the requirements and strategy that drive these things. The strategy includes daily standup meetings, pair-programming, collaborative backlog grooming, demos, and pair programming.

Agile Principle 7

The seventh agile principle focuses on making the working software of an organization the primary gauge of progress. The proponents of the agile philosophy are pretty quick to tell us that the major focus of our business is building software. That's where our time must be spent. Detailed documentation comes secondary to the working software. This mentality channels the products to the markets fast and does not let documentation become a bottleneck.

The best success measure is building and bringing into the market a product that the customers love.

Agile Principle 8

Agile principle eight highlights sustainable development. The developers, sponsors, and users should indefinitely maintain a constant pace. Keeping up with a rapid and demanding release schedule is likely to be taxing for a team if expectations are sky-high. Agile principles make us mindful of this. Therefore they encourage us to set clear and realistic expectations. The idea behind this is to improve the work-life balance and keep the morale high to prevent burnout among members of cross-functional teams.

Before you start a sprint, you should carefully consider the amount of work you should commit to. The development teams are unlikely to over-promise what they are likely or unlikely to deliver. Everyone agrees on what should be done during a sprint. Once a sprint starts, there is no need to add additional tasks. The product managers generally act as the gatekeepers to cut down on the noise from different other stakeholders.

Agile Principle 9

Agile principle nine revolves around regular attention to technical excellence. It reinforces the notion that the good design of a method boosts agility. While the agile philosophy encourages frequent and shorter cycles, it emphasizes keeping things tidy so that they don't create problems in the future. Product managers tend to forget about it because they don't usually spend days researching the project code bases but it still is of the utmost importance for them.

The team should be mindful of the technical debt and its implications of new initiatives and features. Developers and the products ought to work together to understand when the technical debt stays acceptable. The product, on a perfectly regular basis, will have to allocate resources for refactoring efforts.

Agile Principle 10

Agile principle ten revolves around maximizing the work done. You might have heard of the 80/20 principle. This is the concept that you get 80% of your results with merely 20% of work. Agile principles usually encourage thinking in this style.

Product managers have to make highly focused and informed product decisions. They have to align the product strategy with the organization's goals while staying picky about what features and stories actually matter. The short sprints that agile is characterized with tend to offer many opportunities for experimentation and immediate testing. This may help cut down uncertainty whether the initiatives produce predicted output.

Agile Principle 11

Agile principle eleven is about the requirements, architectures, and designs that emerge out of self-organizing teams. In the traditional software development methodologies, you will see team structures in a pyramid format, in which the management has to make key decisions for the contributors. Agile principles suggest that companies should use self-organizing teams, which work on a flat management style. The flat management style encourages decision-making by a group rather than a management team or a singular manager.

Agile Principle 12

The agile principle twelve talks about regular intervals during which the team has to reflect on how the members become highly effective and how it adjusts the behavior. If your company lives by agile principles, there will be no talk about lack of change. Just as we keep learning new things about the markets and the customers, we also learn from different processes we use. Agile does not mean you have to follow strictly defined processes for releases and sprints. Agile revolves around regular and continuous improvement, which extends to the teams and the processes.

Testing and experimentation are not just limited to products. Agile teams have to experiment with the processes by default. You may think you are doing something new, only to experiment with the revised version of all the processes involved and then discover a highly effective method. Experimentation with the team is highly important and equal to experimentation with the software you have been building lately.

Agile Principles at Work

Do you know how to check if the Scrum framework is faring? Is it faring well, or is it not faring well? Since it is named agile framework, you need to look at if the practices that members of the Scrum team and other stakeholders work well while following the agile principles they must follow.

When we talk about the Waterfall system, a plan-driven development works when the challenges that an organization meets remain predictable, adamant about changing, and well-defined. While the Waterfall method, a plan-driven approach, is still relevant and useful for many scenarios, you may consider it a measurable, orderly, and accountable way of initiating a project. However, you will need agile methods when you have the knowledge and awareness that things are unpredictable. That's why certain frameworks such as Scrum adhere to a unique set of principles and practices to address the ever-looming uncertainty. The agile principles can be divided into different types of categories such as the following:

Uncertainty and Variability

Certain agile processes have been properly created to embrace emerging variability that may aid you in creating a better feature. To address the unknown and certain variances, they will pursue the developments and apply the iterations to ensure that they will meet their well-defined goals well in time. When they have embraced variability, they become leverage for adapting during work. They ensure adaptation by bringing in transparency in their processes and by ensuring constant inspection. Variances, too, are destined to become predictable over time because you may feel the need to adapt them frequently upon rising needs.

Adaptation and Prediction

In the agile framework Scrum, you may need to keep your options open. You will also need to accept that it may be possible to produce smooth features in one go. To attain a shippable feature, different frameworks such as Scrum may need to adapt to changes and explore certain possibilities until they consider the changes economically sensible. It means that agile processes ought to balance adoptive work patterns that align with the schedule and work upfront.

Validated Learning

In the agile framework, the people involved in developing a product ought to validate their assumptions. Also, they have to do that faster. They also have to leverage several simultaneous learning cycles to ensure that their work is rendered faster. That's why a well-organized workflow needs to make feedback possible promptly.

The Work-in-Progress Pattern

Work in progress in Scrum refers to the work that the development team has already started, but it has not yet finished. When you are dealing with a work in progress situation, you must stay committed to working in an economically sensible way so that the development teams may finish different batches of work in the required timeframe. Also, you need to stay tuned to whether the work is being finished inside the allocated budget or not. In the agile project management method Scrum, small work batches are mostly favored for promoting the benefits mentioned below.

a. A reduced time cycle: when you divide the work in small windows, it yields fewer tasks that you have to process in a sprint. This means that a team member has to wait for a lesser amount of time if he is waiting for another employee to produce output before he could start working. In this way, everyone in the work chain will work faster and produce faster outputs.

b. Reduced variability in the work flow: when you have to deal with small-sized work in the form of batches, the work batches flow nicely among the team members since they ought to count on resources to accommodate a working batch.

c. Faster feedback: small work windows result in more feedback and faster feedback. You can have more feedback for smaller work windows since you can accomplish them faster, cutting down on the risk factor ultimately.

d. Low overhead: when different teams collaborate and work in smaller batches, they do not need to spend many resources on overhead to complete the cycle.

e. A higher sense of urgency: small work batches mean that it is possible for all who are involved in the process to see the possible causes of mistakes, delays, and developmental progress. Since they have may rectify the blunders and trace their progress, your employees will be highly motivated to finish the work batch they currently have and to get on top of the one that is up next.

When you have considered all these elements, you may be able to effectively compute the costs of the delays by digging into the number of resources you might have lost because of some unfinished work. This allows you to set and change the priorities you have to consider when developing a product. You also have to focus on the idle work, rather than having management upset by some team members sitting idle after finishing their work. By taking a look at the work that still is undone, you will have the opportunity to calculate the costs that went overhead and are likely to lay waste. Also, when you have calculated how much work is to be done, you will have more clarity about delegating your tasks.

Progress

When you use Scrum to manage your projects, you have the power to measure the progress in line with what has already been delivered and validated. This means that you will have the least concern about how much ground your teams have covered in the production phase or whether everything is following a plan or not. When you take a look at the progress from this angle, you are likely to do the following two things.

a. Since there is no plan for you to follow faithfully, you should be aware that things may not go as planned or as expected. When you are working in Scrum, you must make provisions for planning again. As soon as you receive the information, you have to adapt to different changes that have popped up over the past week. The provisions will be highly necessary if you have economically important details that you must consider during the development phase.

b. The second element of measuring progress is calculating how much progress you have made through the proper validation of the work sheets. You can measure your progress when you can create the validated assets that are likely to work. They must deliver a certain value that your end-users and clients need instead of merely meeting the deadlines and strictly working on a budget. Ultimately, you can receive feedback that you must have to identify your next step in the project you are working on.

c. Your processes will fail if your development plan will cease to deliver things of value. Since agile frameworks like Scrum measure progress by calculating the satisfaction or the value, the artifacts may change if the situation has shifted from the view of the customer.

This alludes to the fact that when you start adhering to the agile project management method Scrum, you have to validate the assumptions and then mature them into knowledge of customer value. In the agile project management method Scrum, each artifact that lacks a value to present does not offer any useful assumption to support you in knowing what you must do in the next step.

Performance

There are different work characteristics in Scrum that describe the standards of good performance. You should be aware that you are having excellent performance when you do the following:

a. You are working fast, but you are not working in a rush. While it is perfectly okay to view agile processes as the frameworks that demand swift feedback, the pace of performing work in Scrum does not mean that you have to jump from the first step to the second in the blink of your eye. This only has to happen in a certain scenario that has zero variances. This is desirable and is less likely to happen. When you are using Scrum, your goal is to have fast development while being extremely adaptive and flexible.

b. Time is important for Scrum to work properly since people have been working inside time-boxed sprints. However, you do not need to rush things up in Scrum just to make sure that things are going at a sustainable pace. When you choose to stick to sustainable methods, you are sticking to the idea that you are working at a pace that gives room to work for a longer period. This will prevent you and your team from getting exhausted. This will also keep you from wasting money on undue things. In addition, this will ensure that the quality of the product does not suffer.

c. The traditional frameworks, like the Waterfall method, focus on careful planning. They compel you to do everything as per the standard plan. That's how the

Waterfall method succeeds in producing a high-quality product, but it is extremely important to know what quality is required and what is to be maintained. In the Waterfall method, you cannot know what quality you will produce until you enter the final steps of production. If testing reveals that the product is not of the expected quality at the start, it becomes necessary to carry out the test-and-fix method that consumes time and resources.

In Scrum, there is a cross-functional team that owns of what quality the results are being produced. They usually make it a point that they follow the quality pattern in each sprint during the production phase. When they are working on the increments of the product, everyone remains aware that they do it with confidence. When the product gets ready, it is ready to be shipped right away. You don't need to try test-and-fix methods just because you have alternate quality contrary to what you had expected. Therefore, the risk of spending more to revise the product decreases dramatically.

d. You don't have to observe certain ceremonies as little as possible. Formalities play a mega role in the traditional working processes. In traditional methods, like Waterfall, the success of each phase is measured by three things - the adaptation of the checkpoints, creation of different documents, and the creation of a team that will work on one aspect of the product. This multiplies the costs of possible delays.

In the agile project management method Scrum, organizations cut down on these ceremonies as much as possible. Since there is usually no space for the checkpoint apart from the point where a sprint ends and the team has a meeting with the stakeholders, the work is usually done quickly. Confidence among the stakeholders exists already, and they have knowledge that the features that each sprint has produced will be soon ready for the production phase.

When you have learned these principles, you gain knowledge about how you can turn your organization upside down and mold its procedures as per the procedures and methods of Scrum.

Chapter Six

Product Backlog

The product backlog is basically the list that contains different sets of priorities in a certain project. It is something that gives a shared understanding of what people should create and in what way they must build it. In Scrum, as long as a system is being created, supported, or improved, the product backlog exists.

Product backlog items are features and items that possess a real value for the user or the customer. These items are named user stories. Product backlog items or PBIs fall into the form of defects that must be repaired. They can also be in the form of research or knowledge-acquisition work or technical enhancements. Whether there are efficient or good product backlogs, all of them carry the same traits. These traits are given as under:

These Are Properly Detailed

Not all the PBIs carry the same detail that the Scrum team and the stakeholders are aware of. The PBIs that must be worked on are generally the small ones with much detail to accommodate the nearest sprint. Those that usually are not defined and are not divided yet into smaller tasks are the ones that pertain to the lowest level of the priority list.

The Emergent

The product backlog must not be frozen or must not be seen as a whole when the product is being built, maintained, or repaired. It must regularly be updated in accordance with the information that the organization receives. This means that it will keep updating as frequently as possible when the competitors make quite a bold move to challenge your product. It will keep up the updating process whenever there is poor feedback about a certain feature of the product left by a customer or quite an unforeseen technical issue that pops up along the way. These scenarios may appear to be problematic. However, the product backlog should remain flexible to adapt to the ever-changing scenarios.

Estimation

Each PBI must have a set size that should be equal to the size of the effort, which everyone who is involved in the creation of the product must exert to make it possible. All these estimates will become the most important factors that a product owner considers while setting priorities in the product backlog. Putting an item above the rest to a product owner means that the item has been measured to stay in the working capacity and the organization's budget. It also means that the product owner has foreseen the economic benefits that must be cashed in when the next sprint has been completed.

Priorities

While the product backlog is about setting the project's priorities, you should understand that all items will not be prioritized inside sprints, but it is quite useful for prioritizing PBIs that should belong to the upcoming and foreseen sprints. However, the afterthought features of the product that are usually created and added to the product after its release must not be a part of the product backlog.

Product Backlog Grooming

The grooming of the product backlog refers to the creation and refining of the PBIs. It refers to the estimation of the items of the product. It also refers to the ordering of the items in the backlog as per how prioritized they are.

All the items in the product backlog must be estimated to identify the rank inside the backlog. The items inside the product backlog should be estimated to decide whether the Scrum team must do any additional work to refine the items. At the same time, when some kind of important information jumps in, new items can be formed in the product backlog and then inserted into the list according to their priority.

Whenever you have come closer to a big item, you will have to refine it into little chunks to know how to fulfill it. You might decide that a particular item in the product backlog is unnecessary to consume resources on and, therefore, must be sliced out of the list first. When the product owner, all the stakeholders, and the development team decide to groom the product backlog, they usually opt not to agree on when the grooming should occur. When the work has been initiated, grooming occurs as an out-of-the-flow form of activity since Scrum creates an unpredictable environment where everyone on the team should be ready to inspect the product features produced in sprints. They should also be ready to adapt to certain changes and embrace some good practices whenever it is necessary.

You must take the time to halt the work. Meetings for grooming should only happen whenever they are necessary. Otherwise, it is likely to disrupt the fast workflow of Scrum.

When Will the Product Backlog Be Ready?

When the product owner has completed grooming of the product backlog and the development team is highly confident that they are able to achieve the assigned products in the next available sprint. After that, the product backlog will be ready to review. This means that the product backlog will have satisfied the following criteria.

1. You have clearly stated the business value of all the items.

2. The development team has clearly understood all the details of different items and can decide that they are in a position to complete all the items that the product backlog contains.

3. The development team is appropriately and sufficiently staff for the fulfillment of the product backlog.

4. The PBIs are small, and they are estimated to be completed in sprints.

5. The product owner has already worked up a testable and clear process.

6. The Scrum team has complete knowledge of how they have to demonstrate a certain item during a sprint review.

After fulfilling the above-mentioned criteria, the team ensures that the product backlog is ready to work on. In the next chapter, I will walk you through what responsibilities a Scrum Master plays in the Scrum network.

Chapter Seven

Scrum Master

A Scrum Master, who is popularly dubbed as the servant leader, is usually a motivator, coach, and leader for the agile team. The basic role of the Scrum Master is educating the development team members about the processes of agile project management and helping them follow the standard practice of Scrum in a highly religious manner. A good Scrum Master helps establish top-performing team dynamics, exponential growth in the processes, and an uninterrupted flow in the processes. The Scrum Master plays a central role in the progressive growth of the Scrum team. The Scrum Master has the job of collaborating with the Product Owner, who generally focuses on developing the right product. The Scrum Master also collaborates with the development team that produces the product in the right way. The basic job of the Scrum Master is to help all team members understand the values, practices, and principles of Scrum and, in return, get the best output for the customer in the form of the best product.

A Scrum Master is an expert in the world of Scrum. He or she has the right skills and the ability to coach the development team regarding the principles, values, and processes involved in the Scrum framework. Despite the implications of the post's title, the Scrum Master does not have the authority to make key strategic product decisions. However, the Scrum Master is always accountable for the processes of Scrum and the effectiveness of the development team. Any decisions affecting the overall scope of work fall under the responsibility of the product owner. The Scrum Master has nothing to do with them.

The Scrum Guide has clearly defined what roles the Scrum Master has to play and what values and rituals he has to take care of. The Scrum Master must follow a set of values and rules to get the optimum benefits of the agile processes. The Scrum Master collaborates with the development team, the entire organization, and the product owner. He or she coaches them through the full implementation of the framework of Scrum. Scrum is quite easy to understand, but it is equally tough when the team enters the implementation phase. Mostly, Scrum participants say that they find a new way to use Scrum methods and do not play by the book.

Scrum Master's Roles

Scrum Master's role inside a Scrum framework is complicated. He must play multiple roles like coordinating with the team and consulting each member if everything is going on up to the mark. For his roles in the Scrum framework, he must provide different services to the people he collaborates with.

Scrum Master's Service to the Current Owner

The Scrum Master has to guide the product owner in a number of ways as the following:

1. The Scrum Master helps in formulating different techniques to ensure effective and efficient management of the product backlog.

2. The Scrum Master helps ensure that all the goals, the product domains, and the product scope have been accomplished. All of them must be understood by all members of the Scrum team properly.

3. A Scrum Master aids the development team in reading through and understanding all the items that are parts of the product backlog.

4. He conceives the basic idea to produce a product and then implements the production idea in a completely practical environment.

5. The Scrum Master ensures that the product owner clearly understands the arrangement of the product backlog to yield the optimum and maximum value.

6. He understands the process and the importance of agility in the process.

7. He facilitates different Scrum events when a need arises or when he is requested to do so.

Scrum Master's Service to the Development Team

The Scrum Master plays an important role regarding the work services of the development team.

1. The Scrum Master has the core role of removing certain impediments that come in the way of the performance and productivity of the team.

2. It is the job of the Scrum Master to help the development team create and process high-end products.

3. He facilitates different Scrum events when he is requested to do so by the development team.

4. He trains the development team to feel comfortable working efficiently in organizational environments that are alien or have little knowledge of what Scrum is and how it works.

Scrum Master's Service to the Organization

The Scrum Master has certain responsibilities related to the organization as a whole as well.

1. The first responsibility of the Scrum Master toward the organization is to help the employees and the stakeholders fully understand and implement the best practices of Scrum.

2. The Scrum Master has the role of a change agent to play in the organization. A change agent boosts the productivity of the development team.

3. He has the role of leading the organization in the successful adoption of Scrum methods.

4. He takes part in planning the implementation of Scrum in the organization.

5. He has to join other Scrum Masters to make the application of Scrum highly effective in performing and successfully executing multiple tasks in the organization.

Responsibilities of the Scrum Master

The Scrum Master has some responsibilities on his or her shoulders. Here is a rundown of those responsibilities.

Coach

The Scrum Master must perform the job of a coach to train the product owner. Also, he must coach the development team as well. The Scrum Master will remove the barriers he detects in between different roles in the Scrum network. He will also equip the product owner with all the necessary knowledge and skills to effectively run the product development process. The Scrum Master must stay highly focused on the development team as to what they have been doing. He must carve out the most appropriate way to support the team, so they feel confident of lifting their performance and carrying it to the ultimate level. He must ensure that the development team is fully equipped and well trained so that it may be able to cope up with the challenges that pop up along the way. Like a well-mannered and honest coach, the Scrum Master does not merely take matters into his own hands and start solving problems that the team faces. Instead, he finds out practical ways to facilitate the team in finding solutions to their problems themselves. Only in extreme cases when the team is just unable to find a solution, the Scrum Master jumps in, takes ownership of the escalating situation, and solve the problems accordingly.

Servant Leader

The Scrum Master's other name is the servant leader in the Scrum world. When he is coaching the development team, he acts as their servant because he asks them politely how he can help them. In the Scrum process, a servant leader asks the team what he, in his capability, can do for the team. He has one goal, to boost the effectiveness of the team. Rather than requesting others to help him achieve the goal, he asks them how he can help them. His ultimate goal is to improve the quality of teamwork and the quality of individual work as well. Instead of rebuking and snubbing the team by becoming a master, the Scrum Master must enable, encourage, and energize the team. He must aid them in realizing their inner potential. Take a look at the qualities of the servant leader.

1. A servant leader possesses top-level listening skills.

2. A servant leader is highly empathic.

3. He loves to cultivate a culture and environment of trust among the team members.

4. He loves to act humbly.

5. He likes encouraging other people.

The Scrum Master, as a servant leader, should lead the development team through the debates on conceiving brilliant ideas and through healthy conflicts. He should teach, coach, and mentor the organization and the team in adopting Scrum methods. He should step up to help the development team and prevent the incoming impediments in the way. He should empower and then guide the team members on how to self-manage.

Authority Processing

The Scrum Master must ensure that the development team is fully adhering to the Scrum values and principles. The Scrum Master has to ensure that the development team is improving the production process and the revenue and value. The Scrum Master should not be mistaken with the functional manager or project manager in terms of authority. He does not have the power to hire or fire team members. The Scrum Master lacks the authority to demand from any team member the estimated completion time of a product or a task. He has nothing to do with whether the work is completed or not. Instead of running after the team to get completion dates or getting the work done that is pending, he just has to help them adhere to the standard Scrum processes. Adhering to the processes, in turn, ensures the work is done and the product is delivered to the client on time.

Solution Expert

The Scrum Master has the responsibility of popping out impediments that tend to hamper the team's overall progress. This responsibility is important when team members fail to remove the impediments after several attempts. The timely removal of impediments and availability of solutions boost the overall productivity of the team.

Shield against Interference

The Scrum Master is also dubbed as a protector of the team because he shields them from outside interference that tends to interrupt the product process during each sprint. Interference can arise out of different situations. Managers may interfere in the production process by redirecting the team members to other non-important tasks in the midst of a sprint. The Scrum Master stays ready always to intercepts the interference and shield the team.

Meanwhile, the team must be able to manage the processes. However, most teams that migrate from different other methodologies to Scrum depend totally on the Scrum Master to be their guide in navigating through the agile processes. It takes some time for this responsibility to diffuse itself throughout the team. Here is the gist of some of the key responsibilities that the Scrum Master has to play to complete the projects in time while also maintaining impeccable quality.

1. The Scrum Master has the top responsibility of sprint planning different meetings. He will keep the development team from getting over-ambitious by selecting different product backlog items than they have to deliver. If the Scrum team is immature, the Scrum Master will also help them in the estimating process as well.

2. The Scrum Master will conduct the retrospective meetings, and he will note down the designated areas of improvement that the team had suggested to him. He would also ask others to conduct retrospective meetings to have a different opinion on the improvement of the process.

3. The Scrum Master joins the review meeting and captures the feedback that all the stakeholders raise. He collects the feedback and uses it for taking inputs in retrospective meetings.

4. The Scrum Master does not have to be a part of Daily Scrum, but he has to make sure that the development team conducts the process in a timely fashion. If the development team remains distributed, the logistics team will coordinate the process and produce it for the development team.

5. He has to make arrangements for the Scrum board to be made available for the development team. It can either be a physical board or a digital board on the project management tools that are available inside the organization.

6. He has the job of removing the impediments that find their way to the processes. The Scrum Master must make sure that all the incoming impediments are taken care of and that these impediments do not hamper the development team's performance. Impediments may pop up from different sides. They may come in the form of internal or external blockers

and slow down the pace of progress of the development team.

7. The Scrum Master provides support and guidance to the team. He will regularly guide the team and help them scale up on the success ladder.

8. When working in an organization and a team, internal disagreements inside the team are normal. The disagreements can be due to varying working styles or about the core processes of Scrum. The Scrum Master has the responsibility of ironing out the kinks in the processes and cutting down on the issues. He may arrange one-on-one meetings with the team to understand how he can iron out the problems.

As is the case with all the other team members of the Scrum team, the Scrum Master is not free of mistakes. While it is the fact that anyone can make horrible mistakes and commit gigantic blunders, the Scrum Master makes some common mistakes which he can avoid if he walks carefully.

1. The first mistake that the Scrum Master makes is that he tends to behave like a warden. The project managers who are promoted to the post of Scrum Master find themselves hung up on the command-and-control leadership style. They must behave not like that but as an agile coach. However, they end up becoming wardens who love to handle team members as prisoners of jail. They take over the

responsibility and ownership of the project. In this kind of scenario, the team does not take up the responsibility for their actions. An ideal Scrum Master will only show the right way by which the team may carry out their own job and assume the ownership of products.

2. The second mistake that the Scrum Master makes is thinking that he also is the product owner. No. They are not the same. This does not end up well because these two roles have different focus points. Their roles are different, and both roles need different skill sets. The product owner is called the voice of the customer. He tends to speak in stakeholders' best interest and keeps in view the product that is being prepared. The Scrum Master, on the other hand, stays focused on the long-term effectiveness of the development team so that the team improves itself in delivering some high value to all the stakeholders. The product owner makes sure that the interests of the stakeholders must not suffer. When the product owner and the Scrum Master are the same person, he will tend to pay more attention to the short-term needs of all the stakeholders that will cost him his team.

3. The Scrum Master, sometimes, may be someone who possesses a powerful technical background. He may feel the urge to advise the team members about the solution to different technical issues since he thinks he can provide fast and easy solutions to the team to deal with technical matters. This is not the best way to deal with matters when you are

working in Scrum. The Scrum Master must put full trust in the team to take the most appropriate decision.

Scrum Master Skills

The very first skill that the Scrum Master has is a solid knowledge base. Therefore, a person who wants to become an efficient process coach must have a lot of knowledge about different things. The same is true for the Scrum Master. He must be able to decode technical issues and understand how the team addresses them and how technologies help the team use the end solutions to solve complex problems. For the Scrum Master, knowledge of business domains is good. The Scrum Master is not expected to be an expert on everything, but he should be a person who has some knowledge about everything.

The Scrum Master should also exhibit patience and provide his team sufficient time to arrive at the right answers with their capabilities. At some point, all that ought to be needed is overseeing how the team deals with a particular issue. The Scrum Master must step in when the team appears to be unable to deal with the issues without active support.

The Scrum Master must stay collaborative. As a Scrum Master, you must have the right collaboration skills to work with the development team, the product owner, and the other parties involved in the production process. He should also be willing to collaborate with the ones who might not appear to be involved in the Scrum process. The Scrum Master naturally and technically works as a process coach who helps the Scrum team members achieve their goals.

The Scrum Master should remain transparent in whatever form of communication he or she adopts. When the Scrum Master is working with different team members, there must be no furtive agendas. What you hear from the Scrum Master or see through his gestures or the documents he carries must be the same as what you get in the end. People usually expect nothing less from him. The Scrum Master should be the one who promotes perfectly transparent communication out of the development team. In the absence of transparency, it will be extremely difficult for an organization to inspect or adapt to get the desired results through Scrum. A Scrum Master cannot stop learning ever. He has to keep gaining knowledge to survive and move on.

The Scrum Master is the protector of the Scrum team. He has to make sure that everyone in the team stays on track right from start to finish. He must make sure that the project stays up and running all the time. The Scrum Master should play a central role in creating a balance in the interests between the Scrum roles of the development team and the product owner. He acts as a bridge between the two forces. He must stay cooperative and supportive and maintain the integrity that suits the characters of the Scrum Master. In a typical scenario, the Scrum Master must develop and streamline all the communication channels to ensure that all the products under development must be completed on time and delivered accordingly.

The adoption of agile methods has been increasing globally, and the need for the role of Scrum Master is also increasing accordingly. Several new things are being pinned to the role, and some are being excluded. It is important to stay relevant as a Scrum Master as per the latest needs.

Chapter Eight

Scrum Master vs. Project Manager vs. Product Owner

A s Scrum is accepted as a common method to manage projects across organizations, the roles and responsibilities of the key members are being defined. One of the key members of the process is the project manager. Actually, the responsibilities of a traditional project manager and Scrum project manager have been the focus of many debates lately. In this chapter, I will walk you through the debate and try to highlight the responsibilities of the Scrum project manager.

Traditional Project Management

First, we should look at the role of a traditional project manager to better understand what a Scrum project manager does. Traditional project management was born during the end of the 19th century and the advent of the 20th century. Fredric Taylor and Henry Gantt laid the foundations of traditional project management. Several theories, people, and concepts contributed to developing the concepts and theories of project management. Let us take a look at how many responsibilities were placed on the shoulders of a traditional project manager.

1. He had to ensure that the project must meet all the objectives at the end.

2. He had to estimate the entire scope of products his team had to develop.

3. He must manage the change that ought to arise in the scope.

4. He had to estimate the total time and resources that would be spent on developing the product.

5. He must manage and mitigate certain risks as well.

6. He had to prepare plans and sequences for all the activities and schedules of the project.

7. He had the responsibility to negotiate regarding work matters with the team.

8. He had to eliminate the impediments and assist the rest of the team members.

9. He had to serve as a focal point for all the information that flew across the team.

10. He was responsible for managing the communication of all the stakeholders.

11. He had the onus of tracking down the documentation, reporting everything, and keeping up the documentation.

All these are standard project manager responsibilities, and they are going to vary from one organization to another.

When the world entered the early 1990s, it had become apparent that the traditional Waterfall method was not going to work on bigger projects. It would not work for the software development teams because it could not accommodate certain changes popping up after the design phase. Unfortunately, one of the key tactics that organizations employed to solve this problem was to encourage project managers to double down on micro-managing practices. Many people in software development saw traditional project management systems as the apple of discord.

Enter Scrum

As a result, the Scrum guide did not give room to the post of project manager. Instead, it introduced a very new designation. One of the few reasons Scrum was adopted as the most common agile software development system was its maturity. It approached the process of software development, including the project management aspect of the system. It reassigned the classical responsibilities of a traditional project manager to both the product owner and the Scrum master.

The role of the product owner in Scrum has taken the majority of product-related, business-side responsibilities while the Scrum master focuses mainly on the responsibilities that cater to the needs of the development team. Both roles also have some additional responsibilities, but it is extremely important to notice how they are going to take on the ones that the project managers traditionally handled.

In many organizations that are now practicing the agile project management Scrum, the traditional project managers are the ones who assume two roles. They often play two roles; one is the dual role of Product Owner and Scrum Master on the tactical stage, and the other is of Project Manager on the strategic level. You need to find the perfect balance between the two and move away from traditional systems like getting overly emotional or passionate with the team. Eliminating passion or emotions is one of the biggest challenges people have to face.

Also, keep in mind that in Scrum, some of the responsibilities go into the hands of the team. The development team decides on the total amount of work it must take on in one sprint. The development team also handles how to organize the internal organization of itself. In Scrum, we label the team as highly self-organized.

Project Manager in Scrum

If we speak realistically, we must be realistic and consider the fact that in many situations, a project manager can be a welcome addition to these processes if everyone interacts with him or her in the absolutely right way. Let us take the example of the company that builds software for the customers and also assigns a Scrum team to complete each project. In these kinds of cases, the product owner's role is assumed by a person on the client's side.

In many cases, they are unaware of the implications of this role, which makes it impossible for the team to do the jobs they have been assigned. In this kind of situation, the onus falls on the Scrum Master to educate the product owner.

In practice, the product owner has a short time and willingness to enter the intricacies of Scrum and the new role. They need a person who can coordinate the business side of the project. Unfortunately, Scrum masters are hardly equipped with the right skills to do so. They need someone who can form a bridge between them and the entirety of the Scrum team.

In these types of situations, project managers offer the perfect solution. They support the Scrum team in a fashion that is suitable for Scrum project management. The project manager works in close coordination with the Scrum master to help everyone involved attain what they desire. Project managers in Scrum systems have got a new name for themselves, proxy product owners. They are also called service-delivery managers or vendor-side product owners.

Another case in which a project manager may become an ally of the Scrum team is in complex organizations with enormous bureaucratic structures. In these organizations, Scrum Teams must exist in a certain ecosystem that has been perfectly riddled with governance, politics, regulations, established processes, reporting, documentation, and complex stakeholder structures.

When it comes to theories, the Scrum Master is the only one who has to protect the Scrum team in an ecosystem. A lot of Scrum masters lack the right skills and the right amount of experience to handle this. In some cases, they also have to handle the development work. Even if they are well-equipped with the eight experience and skills, the project manager's responsibilities will consume too much of their time and cause them to neglect certain aspects of the role they have to play.

Scrum Master vs. Project Manager

You might have realized by now that the roles of the two designations are totally different and important as well. Their approaches to work differ. At some point, their roles and responsibilities overlap as well. Let us discuss how many similarities the two have and where they overlap.

1. Both have the job of staying concerned about their teams' performance and finding out how they can improve the efficiency of the team members.

2. The scrum master has to engage with his or her team to facilitate them and coach them, while a project manager also engages their team for an effective resolution of certain conflicts and issues.

3. The scrum master has the primary job of assisting the product owner effectively and efficiently managing the product backlog. On the other hand, the project manager's primary job is seeking input from the clients and all the stakeholders of a product during the development phase.

4. Project managers and Scrum masters need essential skills and experience to master their assigned job.

5. Both roles have numerous challenges to face, and they are in high demand in different types of industries.

6. The scrum master and project manager understand the important quality of the product. Both always have to adhere to the top quality of the work they produce.

The Differences

You may realize that the roles of the Scrum master and project manager tend to overlap. The differences between them far outweigh the similarities between the two roles. Because of the inherent difference between them, the IT and ITES industries choose Scrum master over project manager to achieve their short-term and long-term goals. The challenges that the teams confront in the IT companies vary from the challenges of other industries. You need a highly adaptive model in the IT sector because you do not always know about the requirements when you start the project. The requirements more or less tend to shift during the production cycle. Therefore, it is recommended that you use an incremental, iterative method for your IT industry.

A Scrum master must abide by all the rules of Scrum. He must be the first to endorse the Scrum framework. The project managers have the freedom to customize their methods and approach. They can freely opt for the Waterfall method or use adaptive methods to finalize a product. Whatever suits them for the time being, they use it. Selecting an appropriate approach must be based on what should be a project's demand.

The Scrum Master has the basic job of contributing to resource management and the sectors pertaining to quality management. A project manager contributes his efforts to knowledge sectors.

The Scrum Master must work with small-scale scrum teams. He is held up accountable for a below-average performance of the scrum teams, which are usually smaller in size. On the other hand, the project manager works with big teams. Project managers also need to work with more than one team for managing projects. In comparison, the project manager oversees and reviews the work performance of multiple teams.

Scrum masters are used to facilitating daily meetings of the Scrum team. In contrast, a project manager sets up a meeting calendar and a communication plan, which are quite contrary to what the Scrum master does. Also, the frequency of the meetings to discuss the project's progress is planned and decided by a project manager.

A project manager also sets up a work schedule for the team members and assigns them certain responsibilities. On the other hand, the Scrum master coaches a team and motivates them. A project manager ensures that the schedule and plan for the project are well prepared. In some cases, project managers are also involved in setting up the budget of the project. The Scrum master is concerned about growing the value of the product based on the stories of users.

Both roles demand different sets of skills. Hence they demand a different level of certifications. Both roles remain highly industry-specific. The Scrum master works in the IT industry mostly while a project manager works in a project that may belong to any kind of industry.

Scrum Master vs. Product Owner

In the world of product management, each person in the structure needs to play a specific role. Despite that, people start mixing up the roles of different team members. The role of the Scrum master and the role of the product owner are niche-focused roles. Most non-product people do not have a good idea about what they do. While the Scrum master and the product owner are integral parts of the team, they also need a different skill set to perform their jobs properly.

The Scrum Master is a highly skilled person. The foremost set of skills he or she has to demonstrate is leadership skills. The Scrum master tends to remove the roadblocks that pop up along the way while the team gets on track to achieve a goal. They will discover certain distractions and get rid of them while ensuring that the team is following the standard Scrum practices. They mentor others and possess extremely sophisticated communication skills. They make sure that they collaborate well and mentor well. They demonstrate excellent listening skills. They are always willing to float new ideas and discuss existing ideas. They like to prepare plans and do customer research.

The Scrum Master needs to stay open to certain changes since it is the key part of their job. They must be able to help out other team members in adopting new changes. They should facilitate the process of change. As already mentioned, they should have formal certifications about the process of Scrum and management of products. These skills are process-based skills. Several project managers turn into Scrum masters because the skills are more or less similar.

The product owner is different because the post requires a different set of skills to ace the position in the Scrum network. The product owner must stay committed to the vision. He must be able to communicate that vision to all the stakeholders during the development stage of the product. This also includes explaining certain changes in the product backlog, certain requirements, and other processes that are related to the overall vision of the product.

The development team off and on consults the product owner because product owners clearly understand the product plan. Therefore, they ought to remain available at all times, and they must stay open to communication. Product owners have to show responsibility for the success of the product, and they also need to focus on the production phase. They must be responsible for making sure that ROI must stay positive in the end.

In small companies, the responsibilities of the Scrum master and the product owner may tend to overlap. In large and small companies, they have distinct roles to play. Several smaller companies ask if the product owner can turn into the Scrum master. A clear answer to this question is 'no.' The major reason for this is that this step is likely to create a conflict of interest. The product owner creates and sets the vision for a product. He also plans to produce a refined and successful final product. Scrum masters must oversee the entire process, and they must ensure the process stays relevant and efficient. The Scrum master reviews the product owner's work and provides his recommendations to introduce improvements and best practices in the system. That's why both these jobs demand different people who keep separate perspectives.

Chapter Nine

The Scrum Team

S crum has three roles: the product owner, the scrum master, and the development team. While the roles are crystal clear, what should be done with the existing titles of the job is confusing. Several teams ask if they must change their titles when they have to adopt Scrum. The short answer to this quick question is a 'no.' In this chapter, I will walk you through different Scrum roles and how to fold them into the organization without the printing of new business cards that will cost the company extra money.

Scrum Roles vs. Job Titles

Any job title, even the existing ones, may perform one of these roles. As the essence of Scrum may be empiricism, continuous improvement, and self-organization are the three roles that define the responsibilities of the team. These roles smoothen the process of accountability in the teams and allow them to deliver the work effectively. This also allows the teams to take on the responsibility for how they must organize and how they must keep improving themselves.

How to Build a Scrum Team

Scrum is a framework that teams can use to build up their processes. The framework gives them a basic structure to create their processes and develop products. It gives them the structure to set up regular meetings and artifacts. It also gives them a glimpse into who does what in the process.

Scrum does not give them a one-size-fits-all model to work in an organization. Suppose the team is working on the development of a web insurance application. In that case, they are going to need people who are well-versed in technology, back-end systems, and different domains of business. If the team has been working on Donkey Kong, the skills needed for the team would be completely different from the ones needed for the previous team. They would need a graphic designer, a graphics developer, and a sound engineer. As the basic problems are different, the skills needed and the team structures may also be different.

This gets tougher when the team has a more complex problem to solve. Teams might not know the skills and the amount of work that is needed to be done up front. They may also don't know what level of flexibility they need to change the course once they know the product and the end result.

Scrum gives a lightweight structure with three basic complex roles for the development team member, the Scrum Master, and the product owner to provide some basic structure to the complex, ever-changing, and annoying world.

The Development Team

The development team is the one that does the major work. At first glance, you may think that the development team means engineers, but that's not always the case. As per the Scrum guide, the development team must have people of different kinds such as writers, designers, and programmers, etc.

You may consider it in the same way as a housing project. In the housing project, you need to hire developers. The team of developers initiates and performs the work. This may mean that they need to lay the bricks, perform the plumbing infrastructure work, and dig giant holes for sewerage systems. The person who does the work is known as a developer. This means that the developer's role in the world of Scrum alludes to a team member who possesses the right skills as a part of the development team to perform the work.

The development team ought to be able to be self-organized to make the right decisions to get the work done properly. The development team should be viewed as something that is similar to the production support team that is more often called in at night because something has suddenly gone wrong. The development team, just like the support team during the production phase, makes decisions and also delivers the value for the problem that has popped up recently. Self-organization is not akin to disrespecting an organization. It is rather about the empowerment of the people closest to the work that is to be done. It is about providing these people with the right knowledge and tools to solve the problem efficiently. Here is the rundown of the responsibilities of the development team.

The foremost responsibility of the development team is the delivery of the work through a single sprint. The second responsibility is ensuring transparency during the sprint. To achieve this objective, they set up daily meetings. The daily meeting is known as standup meetings. The daily Scrum offers transparency to work, and it also provides a dedication for the team members to get help, discuss success, and highlight the blockers and the relevant issues. The Scrum Master has the responsibility to facilitate the daily standups. However, the Scrum master's job is limited to only arranging the standup meetings. It is the job of the development team to run the meeting successfully. The meeting is aimed at helping the team so that they can inspect and adapt to the changing needs of the job they have to perform. This makes them more effective and efficient.

The Product Owner

The agile teams are responsive and flexible by design. It is the responsibility of product owners to ensure that they deliver the highest value. The business is usually represented by the product owner, who informs the development team what is important to be delivered early. The element of trust between these roles is extremely crucial.

The product owner must understand customers and have a clear vision about the Scrum team's value to deliver to customers. The product owner balances the needs of different stakeholders in an organization.

The product owner must receive all the inputs and set up the priorities for the work to be done. This is the most important responsibility of the product owner because unclear directions and conflicts of interest will cut down the effectiveness of the development team. It will also break up the level of trust in the relationship among team members.

Agile teams are structured as such to inspect and adapt. This means that a shift in the priority leads to a sea change in the team structure and work-related products. It will also bring a mega change in the result. Therefore, the Scrum teams must designate a person who sets up the priorities. That person is designated as the product owner.

The Development Team Structure

The development team is an integral part of a mega Scrum team. The development team consists of professionals who deliver a releasable increment of 'Done' product when a sprint ends. During the Sprint Review, the 'Done' increment is usually required. Only the key members of the development team usually create the increment. The development team in Scrum is very well-structured and is empowered as well by the organization to manage their own work. This practice results in a unique synergy that will optimize the efficiency of the team.

The Ideal Size

There is no standard size for the development team. There is no mention of how large the team should be. The size of the team may vary from one Scrum team to another. A development team should be small enough to stay agile, and it should be large enough to finish a large amount of work in the specific sprint. This is going to produce the product of the maximum possible value.

If the team consists of less than three members, the total number of interactions in the team will be logically going to be less. This will also result in clear low productivity levels. Extremely small development teams may encounter some skill constraints during ongoing sprints. In these cases, they will not deliver a releasable increment. On the other hand, an extremely large-sized team is also not good for developing a good product.

If the size of the Scrum development team is more than nine members, you may experience some serious coordination problems. In addition to this, extremely large development teams tend to generate very unnecessary complexity. The empirical processes are the least used in these cases. It needs to be noted that the Scrum master and the product owner are out of this total count unless they actively perform work for a Sprint Backlog. So, the number should be calculated carefully.

Characteristics of the Team

There are some key characteristics of the development team that you must consider. The most important of the characteristics are given as under:

1. The first key characteristic of the development team is that they are a self-organized team. No one in the Scrum

network, not even the Scrum master himself, can direct the team members to convert the product backlog into increments of releasable functionality. They do everything on their own, and they must know how to do it on their own.

2. The development teams are cross-functional. The team consists of members who possess a variety of skills. As a team, these skillsets, when combined, are necessary for a product increment.

3. The members of the development team do not carry individual titles. They work as a coherent whole. Each member of the team is identified as a part of the team. His or her relationship with the team works irrespective of the work he or she performs in the team. All are equal. There is no one above others.

4. There is absolutely no place for sub-teams in the Scrum network. The development team exists as a single whole. There are no factions. Although the team may have business analysis domains, operations, testing, and architecture, it works as a whole, not in groups.

5. The development team has full accountability for the project and not of the individual team members. If the product is faulty, the onus lies on the team as a whole. You cannot point out single members and place responsibility for whatever wrong happened to the product.

Development Team's Responsibilities

Here is a rundown of some of the key responsibilities that the development team has.

Performing Spring Execution

The foremost responsibility of the development team is to perform the execution of the sprints during the development phase of the product. When the sprint is being executed, the development team members perform different tasks like designing, integrating, building, and testing the product backlog items into increments of shippable functionality. The development team self-organizes and decides mutually how to plan, execute, and communicate the work to achieve this. The development team spends a handsome amount of time performing the execution of sprints.

Qualities

The development team in Scrum has some key qualities that make them distinguished in front of other teams.

The development team believes in pair programming. The first job of the programmer in the development team is working in close collaboration with the others at the same workstation. One programmer, known as the driver, has to write the code while the other, known as the navigator, has to review each line of code.

Each member of the development team needs to be well-versed with some really advanced tricks and techniques up his or her sleeve. The techniques should be about using automated unit tests to drive design software and do away with the team's dependencies.

In the development team, self-motivation is considered a virtue. It is the greatest driver of efficiency. It is the one that usually is seen in successful development teams. There is nothing like a junior hierarchy within the development team. The team always has to work on its own. A member that cannot maintain self-motivation cannot survive in the Scrum environment.

The basic foundation of teamwork inside the development team is that each member should be a team player. The foundation is built when the efforts of all the individual members of the development team are summed up into a coherent whole up to the point that you cannot distinguish one person's efforts from another's. That's how the development team sets itself on the road to achieving bigger goals while working in extremely close collaboration with other members. The individuality of team members must be eliminated before the members start working on a project.

So, the development team in Scrum is very different from other teams. The requirements of team members, the characteristics, and the qualities of the team differ by a big margin. Not everyone can be a member of the development team in Scrum.

Chapter Ten

Work Estimation

When you start to manage or plan how to plan and build a product, you should answer some key questions before entering the planning phase. The questions may be something like how many features should be included in the product, when will you be able to finish all the work, and how much budget will be used by all the tasks combined?

In order for Scrum to answer these questions, you may need to get a clear estimate of the total size that you may require to build as well as gauge the velocity at which you may be able to get the work done. Once you have acquired the details, you are highly likely to calculate the time that is needed for the development of the product. Also, you will be able to calculate the overall cost of the project.

Cost of Work

You can calculate the product development duration by following a simple formula that I have given below.

Estimated size of features / the velocity of the team

The estimated size of features is the total size estimate of each product backlog item in the development phase in the formula. The second team's velocity is the amount of work that the Scrum team finishes in a single sprint. The velocity is measured by the addition of the size estimates for PBIs that have been accomplished during each sprint.

What to Measure

The relative size measure can be executed to calculate the total amount of work that has been done. Since the items in the product backlog are dubbed as stories, the estimated size of effort that must be done to complete a certain feature is known as story points. You may also get relative size measures by sifting out the ideal days to perform work. See how you can perform the measurements.

The Story Points

The story points in Scrum are the numbers that have been assigned to a specific item in the product backlog, which allows the relationship of different items that must be accomplished. If you have to carve out a title for the project, it may contain a story point of two. Acquiring all the details for publicity copy for the project demands a story point of eight. This means that the effort that should be put into the research phase for publicity is usually four times bigger and massive as compared to what went into the creation of the title.

The Ideal Days

Ideal days are usually the total number of days that you need for a particular PBI. You must take note that ideal days may not be a consecutive number of days on a calendar. It represents the total number of days a person must have to create a story and work on it. The days are not the same as elapsed time. You may take a football game as an example. There are four quarters in the football game. All four quarters of a football game are supposed to last just for 15 minutes. It takes the entire game three full hours to complete the play. By measuring the total work done as per the ideal days, you get enough room for any possible interruptions and distractions that may pop up in any sprint that you have already planned or have been planning for a while.

The question is what you should use as a measure in your organization. There is nothing right or wrong as an answer to this question. You have to find out the best method and the most viable course of action. If there is absolutely no reason to mistake the idea of a person about what ideal days are, you can adopt this measure without any problem. If you think there may be a misunderstanding when you must use the same term, you may need to stick to the use of story points.

Planning Poker

Planning poker is a special technique to measure the PBI sizes. In this special method, you will use a technique that naturally relies on the consensus to have a clear estimate of the efforts that you must exert for each PBI. The product manager must consult experts in the field to expose certain assumptions about the possible effort. He must consult knowledgeable people to produce a system in which everyone related to Scrum gets a clear understanding of how much work is needed to produce the ideal product in the end that satisfied the needs of the end-user.

In the planning poker, the Scrum team is supposed to work in close collaboration so that they may be able to group certain items in the product backlog that carry a similar size. Afterward, the team is likely to use the details they have gotten from the planning poker to estimate other items in the backlog.

There are certain numbered cards used in the planning poker method. The numbers are properly ordered through the Fibonacci sequence. Some of the cards show the relationship between different sizes for a PBI. When you get to see a certain set of numbers on the planning poker, you should be able to read them as the following:

a. 0 – the items are done, or the item is too small and cannot be assigned to a number.

b. ½ - the item is too small.

c. 1, 2,3 these are the points assigned to all the items in the product backlog.

d. 5,8,13 – these are the points that are assigned for the medium-sized items. Several teams look at 13 points worthy item would be of the biggest size of an item that they can put into a sprint. If a certain item scores over 13, they would need to be broken into tiny items instead.

e. 20, 40 – these points are assigned to larger items. Organizations call these story items theme-level stories or features.

f. 100 – these points are assigned to a larger story that is also called an epic.

g. ? – this shows that a certain team member is unable to comprehend what the item actually is. This shows that the product owner is being asked to clarify or define it.

h. π - this symbol does not mean the pi in mathematics. It rather means that somebody on the team wants a break during work to eat a pie or something like that. Some of the decks also use a coffee cup instead of the pi symbol for break. When someone raises the pi card, it means they need an immediate break from work.

There are some rules to follow for planning poker. Here is a list of them so that you can remember them and follow them accordingly.

1. The first rule is that the product owner must read the PBI to the entire team before starting the work on the product development.

2. The second rule is that the development team should discuss each item and ask for the clarifications it needs from the product owner.

3. The third rule is that each member of the Scrum team should select a card representing his or her work estimate. Each member must keep his or her card in hiding from the other teammates.

4. The fourth rule is that once all team members have selected their respective cards, they should simultaneously show those cards to expose what their private estimates of work are.

5. The fifth rule is that if every person on the team has shown their card, a consensus must be reached. The number on each card would be an estimate of PBI.

6. The sixth rule is that if a team member shows a different card, the team must discuss the assumptions or any kind of misunderstanding about PBI. The discussion kicks off usually with the question as to why a person who has already shown a different card made an estimate.

7. When the discussion reaches its logical end, you need to repeat the third step until you reach a consensus among the team members.

Velocity

The term velocity refers to the total amount of work that is completed in a single sprint. It is measured normally by the addition of the sizes of PBIs that are completed at the end of each sprint session. The numbers that are to be added do not include any kind of partially done PBI since they do not get value from it.

Due to this specific definition, Velocity is the way to gauge the output and not the specific outcome or the total value of what should be delivered. It is the way for the team to calculate the number of sprints they must make to complete everything on the product backlog and get the fully discussed feature released.

It is also how to determine each member's total capacity to show his or her commitment to work over the next sprint. That's why the team's velocity is considered a very useful diagnostic system that the Scrum team uses to introduce improvements in the work culture and evaluate how the Scrum system is working to deliver fine results. That's how the development team can expect what end result will be expected of a product and what the end-users need. This is the key to the super successful development of a product. By evaluating the team's velocity, the team has the opportunity to see how the change of process affects the delivery of an item that displays a measurable value to customers.

Velocity Range

When you plan a sprint, you may benefit from the expression of the particular range by saying that your team is most likely to accomplish about 30 to 40 points in each sprint. In this way, you may remain highly accurate in the estimation, and you do not have to stick to a time when PBIs can be easily accomplished.

To measure the range of the velocity, you have to take two velocities from the team members, which becomes your estimation of the faster velocity and the slower velocity of the team. You can calculate and reach an estimate as to when your team needs to do a greater number of sprints on the slower velocity. If the team works by using Scrum for a pretty long period, it would be much easier to make predictions about the future velocities. If there are any new members on your team, there may be occasional discrepancies in the forecast.

One brilliant way to reveal the team's velocity is to make them perform a particular sprint planning to reveal what PBIs the team may commit to in one sprint. If the commitments are found to be reasonable, you may add the sizes of the PBI commitments and then make use of the forecasted velocity.

Since you may need to know the velocity range, you may have the team plan at two variable points. You can use one number of velocity as high and the other one as low. You can introduce some adjustments once you can measure the real range of velocities and use it as the historical velocity of your team.

Most people who stare at the Scrum agile project management method believe that a team's velocity is always bound to improve with time. The trend has its foundation on the logic that if a team inspects and adapts constantly and assumes good practices in the process, the velocity must shoot up after a couple of more sprints.

While the teams may have that aggression to improve and focus on delivering quality features with a low level of technical debt, it is completely logical to issue judgments that the velocity needs to improve. However, the trend will not always be toward an upward trajectory. In some cases, it is bound to go down.

This does not mean that when the team's velocity drops, it no longer has the potential to improve its velocity. There is more than one way to improve the team's velocity, like the activation of new policies that cut down the distractions or create certain provisions for the technology to jump in and improve the development time. The introduction of these changes means that the team's velocity is likely to drop for the time being, and then it will improve and see an upward trend once the team is used to new changes.

Some organizations say that they tend to improve their development time by making their teams take overtime shifts but with this new thinking, certain risks are attached. While I believe that the velocity of the team may be likely to improve during the first few instances of the overtime that the organization allocates to the members of the team, it is possible that the range of the velocity drastically drops and the quality of the product suffers after some consecutive shifts of overtime by the company.

When you have to determine the factors that boost the team's velocity, you may need to find out the best methods that exert long-term effects on the organization's future course.

Misuse of Velocity

Velocity is considered a very good planning tool. It is viewed as the best in the diagnosis of the metrics of the team. However, it is not the best performance metric that gauges the productivity of the team. When velocity is specifically used in a particular organization as a productivity gauge, it takes up the position of motivating bad behaviors in performance terms.

Suppose you have already made a point to issue a mega performance bonus to a specific team that possesses the best velocity. In that case, you might think that it is fitting to reward a wonderful and productive work behavior. But if you compare teams in terms of velocity range and not by the size of PBIs that they have been looking after in sprints, especially if team A is faster than team B, then it would depend on how both are taking the same size of tasks. Whether they are working on them with the same approach or they are taking a different course of action. For example, team A may allocate a PBI a story point 2 while the other may feel that it should be given 20.

At the same time, a team's velocity range may be judged as per the definition of done to produce a fine product or feature and not just to meet the high velocity. While different teams must improve on the total numbers that they are getting in a specific duration, the organizations must keep motivating the teams to reduce the technical debt if it exists.

You must consider velocity as to how it may assist in the development of a product. You can use it by deploying the right course of action, accurate planning, and pondering and finding out the best way to how velocity will help out teams for the promotion of development in the groups. Otherwise, it would fail to promote development in the groups and succeed in promoting development in the team's behaviors, which would be wasteful for the organization.

Chapter Eleven

In-Depth Scrum

Scrum teams are the best assets of each Scrum-based organization. By properly structuring them and then making sure that they are working well with one another, you may guarantee that the Scrum-based project you have been running will achieve success. So what will happen if your organization plans to release multiple products?

If you are trying to create a single product with one deadline for the release you have been trying to meet, you need to build a cross-functional team. If you work using the Scrum framework for a longer time period, you need your Scrum team to become a top-performing group that will eventually produce a high value for the business.

You are highly likely to experience exponential growth in the organization. This will need you to manage more than one Scrum teams, which will eventually intersect with others to generate greater business value.

Component vs. Feature Teams

When you have a feature team, you have a cross-component and a cross-functional team that will eventually create the final features from the product backlog. A component team stays focused on the development of subsystems or key components that will be utilized in the creation of one part of the end-user feature.

For this reason, the component teams are known as the asset teams. Similar skills bind these people together. The members of these types of teams are likely to report to a manager and then use some centralized resource that different others share as well. Many organizations highly favor building teams to put all the experts at work and then produce a certain part of a product until each component is finalized and assembled quickly.

The problem with the component teams is that they must rely on other teams to work on a particular feature. There is absolutely no way you may run a business with the typical thinking that production must be put on a halt because other component teams are just not done with their share of work. In this kind of situation, the ide component team will not be the one who will have to compensate for the lost time, and the entire business will compensate for that.

Scrum gives its favors to the feature teams, while most other organizations that run on the traditional framework are likely to favor the component teams. Traditional organizations tend to think when there is someone unfamiliar with the production process of the code, then the likelihood of running an error is extremely high.

When there is more than one team concerned with the components that they have to deliver, you may probably predict that the teams will prioritize their backlogs and run the risk that the feature under development is likely to see a logical end.

Its reason is that the more component teams you possess, the higher the failure points that exist in creating the feature. Since Scrum tends to dictate that you must keep one feature team, you will have to be concerned about just one failure location. The solution to this particular problem is creating feature teams that are fully capable of cross-functioning because they have acquired the right skillsets to produce a variety of end-user features without worrying about supplying different pieces of one feature to multiple component teams.

Soon, you will be creating more developed feature teams that will be fully capable of becoming trustworthy custodians of product features instead of hiring experts that will only work on one component. To produce feature teams, you must establish a coherent and logical approach that allows your company to get into the transition to creating multi-feature teams that will eventually manage logistics in producing and finalizing the feature.

Feature Team Production

Suppose your organization consists of more than one component team that carries varying priorities. In that case, you are in a position to create feature teams that will exhibit the skills that you want to shape up and finalize a specific feature. The component teams that have already set up themselves to be trustworthy in achieving their specific tasks may remain for the maintenance of the integrity of a specific individual component. You can assign one member of the component team to serve as a member of the feature team to ensure that the component teams have been working with one another to meet all the needs of the product feature.

Component team members that will serve as feature team members have some key roles to play that are given as under:

The component team member will act as a pollinator. The team component will provide the feature team members with the right amount of knowledge that they usually share in the component team. He shares the ownership of the knowledge and allows shared ownership within the feature team.

The component team member will act as a harvester. He will collect the changes that the feature team must make in the component areas. He has to make sure that the component team knows the changes it needs to make to meet the requirements of the feature team. When the component team comes to the table to discuss the changes, the team will ensure that they must avoid mounting conflicts. To achieve this purpose of evading any conflict, they must make sure that the tasks remain coherent with the feature team backlog.

If you are running a big organization that carries about 50 component teams, you may think you need to put about 50 people in the single feature team. This strictly goes against the tradition and spirit of Scrum, which clearly says that it is against the build-up of large teams. If you run multiple teams that tend to intersect by creating a single feature, you are in a position to produce multiple feature teams and then divide the total number of component teams among them.

In this way, you can form different feature teams around smaller groups of component teams and then promote better coordination in the groups as well. Suppose your organization keeps small-size groups, and it no longer makes sense that you can assign one of the members to a respective feature team. In that case, you are likely to reduce the products in the simultaneous production phase or hire more employees who are experts in a single component area.

There is no single solution that an organization may use when it is solving the problem of the creation of feature teams while at the same time maintaining multiple component teams. Large-sized Scrum organizations that have been highly successful over time adapt to the blended models, which have multiple feature teams at their foundation. Then they produce the component teams when they are needed.

Multiple Teams

In Scrum, you can develop scalability not by creating large development teams but by creating more than one Scrum team that has the right number of people. When you have multiple Scrum teams, you may need to create a specific method about how these teams may coordinate in the first place. You may use the following techniques to accomplish that.

SoS

SoS is the short form of Scrum of Scrums. You already know now that the development teams usually perform daily Scrum when they are performing a sprint execution. To coordinate more than one team and make sure that the members are committed to keeping backlogs that would work really well, the teams may perform an SoS.

In the coordination technique, the teams need to opt to send off a particular member of the team and their ScrumMaster, which may be shared by two or more than two Scrum teams, to the Scrum on the Scrums. Nonetheless, they must ensure that those who attend the SoS are not too big a number.

When the SoS is conducted, the members give answers like what has the team achieved after the last meeting that might affect the other functional teams. They may seek answers to the questions like what the team will do between the current and the next meeting that will affect other teams. And what problems the teams currently face need resolving with the help of one of the other teams in the system.

Like the daily Scrum of an individual team, the SoS may be timeboxed just to be completed in a short time of 15 minutes. However, the SoS may extend beyond this particular time if the teams opt for collective problem solving before moving on to the corresponding sprints.

Release Train

A release train is traditionally a coordination period that is highly useful when you have to align the planning, the visions, and the interdependence in the feature teams. With the help of this method, the synchronization of the cross-team happens, which ultimately allows the teams to get a flexible and fast flow, especially when they are tasked to achieve a bigger product.

The key term 'train' refers to a published schedule about when the agreed-upon features will leave the station. All the team members who will participate in product development must fulfill the product backlogs or place the cargo on the train at a fixed amount of time. Scrum will make it a definite point that all the cargoes will find their way into the train at the right time. If the team misses the schedule, there is no reason to panic since a second train will get to the station at its set schedule.

A highly effective release of the train will follow a set of rules, and if it misses out on the rules, you will see unexpected results.

1. The planning phase will be frequent and periodic, and the release dates of solutions must be fixed. The schedule and quality for the shippable increments (PSI) are fixed, but the scope may vary.

2. The teams must apply the same lengths for iteration.

3. The objective, the global, and the intermediate milestones must be put in place.

4. The PSIs should be available at constant intervals for the system-level quality analysis, reviews of customers, and internal reviews.

5. The system-level iterations' use will remain available for cutting down the technical debt. It will also be available for the teams to get more time for release-level validation and testing.

6. Some of the infrastructure components track before time to allow build up on the existing constructs.

7. A regular system's iteration is usually implemented at different levels.

You can divide a big enterprise backlog into different levels like portfolio backlog, program backlog, and team backlog. The portfolio backlog uses epics to deal with portfolio management, while the program backlog deals with program management and its features. The team backlog deals with product owners who have user stories that can be worked out in sprints. By using Scrum of Scrums, you are in a position to coordinate and properly integrate different tasks belonging to the feature teams that fall into the feature area. You also can integrate their respective jobs in each sprint.

Whenever you find it practical, you should ensure testing and integration across the feature areas. Some teams want to use the last sprint to transfer their work to a train to save some time to harden the developments over the previous sprints and integrate and test results from across several feature areas. When you think that the teams have matured, you should consider that they should cut down on their needs for hardening sprints.

Chapter Twelve

Why Scrum Is the Best Option For Developers

Scrum is the best framework for developers, and there are solid reasons to back this claim. It helps them stay organized, in control, and produce the best product.

Development Team Is in Control

The development team decides the number of items that are selected from the product backlog for a sprint. By this, you can gauge how much power the development team has in its hands. Many believe that product owners must determine his or her plan for the upcoming sprint, but this is no longer the case. The Scrum Team has to decide the goal of sprints while the development team has to determine the number of items for the upcoming sprints. The development team remains in full control of its powers.

Building Increments

As you have already learned in the previous chapters, not even the Scrum Master is in control of the situation. He cannot tell the team how to turn the product backlog into increments that have releasable functionality. This is clearly written in the Scrum guide 2017. The product owner remains the leader of what should be built, but often there are different ways to achieving this. The development team also determines the how-to factor.

The product backlog is in the form of an ordered list of commonly known things to be included in the product. It remains the single most common source for changes that must be made to a product. This alludes to the fact that the team has just the product backlog to take care of to understand what they have to work on in the next phase.

The product owner remains in charge of managing the product backlog. No one, except the product owner, will determine the accurate order of the product backlog items. With this, he or she remains the only one who must discuss with the team what is to be done next.

Focus and Teamwork

The sprint goal helps the team to gather focus on what must be achieved. It basically enables the development team to coordinate to plan toward the sprint goal and help them manage distractions. A top sprint goal is highly important to turn an average sprint into a success.

Skillful Team

The development teams, as per the Scrum guide, are cross-functional. They possess the right skills that a team must have to produce an increment. In Scrum, the development team is not required to depend on outsiders for the creation of the increment. All the required skills can be traced inside the team.

Mutual Understanding on Completion of Increment

When an increment or a product backlog item is described as Done, all must keep in mind what the term Done means. This is a typical definition of the term Done that is used for accessing the work when it is completed on product increment.

After the clear definition of the term Done, it is clear to the product owner, the development team, and the stakeholders that the work has been completed on an increment. With this, everyone gets on the same page during the increment assessment to discuss what should be done next.

Right Thing

Scrum is a framework that people use to address complex adaptive issues while creatively and productively delivering different top value products.

Scrum is created to focus on the delivery of increment that may possess the highest value at a certain point in time.

Chapter Thirteen

Running Multiple Projects

As most organizations need to produce over one product at a particular time, they may need to create choices that may appear to be economically sensible whenever it is time to manage different product portfolios. To do that, they must step up to create management and governance systems that work well with the core agile methods to prevent the disconnection from the agile approaches executed at the individual product levels. In this chapter, I will walk you through how different organizations may strategize portfolio planning and how they can determine if teams may accommodate the additional work.

Decoding Portfolio Management

Portfolio management is often used to determine which type of backlog items in the portfolio that the organization should work on. In creating a plan, the managers who are likely to determine the priority order of PBIs must work on them. When you are conducting portfolio planning, you must consider the following aspects to ensure that the teams can work on the backlog items of your portfolio.

Timing

The very first to keep in consideration is timing. Planning of the portfolio is a marathon activity in an organization. It goes on end until the team reaches a consensus on finalizing the product. As long as the product is in the development phase, you must maintain and manage a portfolio. Since the planning of a portfolio demands proper dealing with the collection of products and is quite bigger in size than the individual portfolios, the managers ought to consider fresh products that they have to take into the portfolio. This does not allude to the fact that portfolio planning must be above product planning. By using the data that is collected during product envisioning, portfolio management enables you and makes it possible for your team to know if it is right to fund a product. You will also get to know what the right way to prioritize items in the portfolio backlog is.

Portfolio planning is not only concerned with the envisioned product only. Reviews should regularly happen on products in the development phase already or in the production phase, or are currently being sold.

The Participants

As portfolio management tends to deal with in-process and newly launched products, the planning participants will include the product owners of internal stakeholders and products. The addition of technical leads and articles may be a welcome addition to your planning team.

The stakeholders ought to have sufficient business perspective to enable them to make the right decisions when it arrives at prioritizing items in the portfolio backlog and what must happen to the in-process products. Some organizations choose to form a stakeholder approval committee to look after the planning process of the portfolio.

Product owners are usually needed in the portfolio's planning phase to see that their products remain prioritized in the portfolio backlog. How the management of the portfolio decides how they would advocate the key resources needed to create the products they have ownership of.

The Process

When you are executing portfolio planning, you will have two outputs; one is the portfolio backlog that is a list of items for all the future products set as per priority, and the other is the set of activities that are basically new products that have been approved and decided for the development phase right away. If you want to control what output should be obtained, you should take care of the following aspects of the process.

Scheduling

The first aspect to take care of is scheduling, which refers to having a great plan when it is about determining the sequence of different products that must go in the portfolio backlog. With the help of this plan, there will come a consideration that the organization possesses limited resources for producing products most economically. On the one hand, while there are many strategies for planning the sequence of the product in the portfolio backlog, the following three strategies will turn out to be effective for the organization.

1. You should focus on making schedules that have been properly optimized for the lifecycle profits. The key here is making the right decisions on which variable you should measure to see if the optimization efforts have been working or not. When you are in the midst of creating scheduling strategies, you may feel the need to take a look at the trade-offs that are a part of the decisions by using standard units of measure, that is considered the lifecycle profit. In this key strategy, you would have the opportunity to schedule different items in the portfolio backlog to properly maximize the lifecycle profits.

2. Lifecycle profits are basically a combination of all profits of a particular product in its entire life. When it comes to portfolio planning, you should be more interested in optimizing the entire portfolio for profit instead of setting your focus on one product. As you are the least interested in making a single product a success, you may feel the desire to hunt down the sequence of backlog items that are likely to post the most profits.

When you are making an educated assessment of the profits, you need to consider two variables: the cost the delays have incurred, and the other is the cost of the overall duration. You can use the following scheduling strategies based on the above-mentioned variables.

The cost of delay remains the same across all the products; however, different products have varying sizes. You need to take first the job that has the shortest duration.

The cost of delay also varies from one product to another, but different products have the same sizes. You need to take out the high-delay cost before others.

Both the cost of size and delay tend to vary among different products. You must take the shortest job first.

Cost of Delay

When you are sequencing items on portfolio backlog, you have to work on some of the products over others. You must keep in mind that the products you are delaying to be worked on later will start at a delay and have a delayed delivery schedule. These delays have a cost to pay. When you are on the way to determining the right schedule for a portfolio product backlog item, you have to answer the question as to what should be the cost of delay in the lifecycle profits when you choose to delay the product development by a set number of days or months? Once you know the exact number of days and months your product will delay, you can calculate the overall cost you have to bear.

When you closely analyze this specific strategy, you will realize that it is not always the right thinking to take on the high profitable

117

item first. If you are working on a project alpha that is giving you 20% ROI and you also have a project beta that gives you back 15% ROI, you will immediately think that you have to take care of the project alpha in the first place, but your planning must not stop here. Suppose you have the knowledge that delay in project alpha means that you will lose $50,000 and delaying project beta will cost you $70,000. In that case, you will realize the gigantic discrepancy in the cost of delay between the two products will ultimately affect the overall profitability of the portfolio.

So, how will you calculate the cost of the delay? When you choose to calculate it, you need to consider the following product attributes and then assign a specific value to the cost of delay. The number 1 value will be the lowest, and the number 10 will be the highest.

a. The first attribute is the user value. It is the potential value that, according to customers, a product has.

b. The second attribute is time value. It alludes to the fact how a customer's perceived value of any product tends to decay with time.

c. The third attribute is related to opportunity enablement on cutting down the risk factor. It is about the value in relation to taking a certain advantage of the mitigating risks and concerning opportunities.

The total cost of delay for a product is usually equal to the total of the costs of individual delays. If you think that there is a lack of fixed value that you may assign for the cost of individual delays, you should create a product delay portfolio to determine the scheduled decisions. You may use the following profile descriptions.

1. The first is known as linear. In this description, the product will carry a cost of delay that is going to increase at a constant rate.

2. The second is a large fixed cost. Here, the product will be accumulating a specific one-time cost if it is not immediately done. This is going to happen if you receive a big payment portion after you deliver a product.

3. The third is the fixed date. The product must be delivered at a specific date in the future. There will be zero delay costs until the date arrives and the product still is in the development stage.

4. The fourth is logarithmic. Here the cost of the delay in product development remains the highest at an earlier time. The cost is going to have a lesser incremental cost after some additional delays.

5. The fifth is intangible. Here the product does not have an obvious delay cost for a very long period. However, you are going to experience a very high cost of delay at an unexpected time.

Inflow Strategies

The inflow strategies deal with the way an organization balances the rate at which the portfolio backlog items are pulled out of inserted. Having a strategy means that you will get to see if the additions to the portfolio backlog are causing any kind of bottlenecks or not. You will be balancing the number of products that are coming out in small but highly frequent releases.

When you have developed a product vision that is in line with the information you require to produce some product with high confidence levels, you feel at ease while deciding whether you need to fund development for a specific product. When you get ready to do this, you will create a proper economic filter to see if it will meet the funding requirements of an organization.

Each organization needs to create some sort of economic filter in line with its funding policies, so you know that you have got on if you can quickly tell that you need to approve a specific opportunity because it is going to deliver a brilliantly overwhelming value as compared to the development cost. If you have achieved some certainty, there will be no talk about if a project that is being laid out needs to be developed.

An organization may desire to put in place a steady stream of products that may enter and leave the portfolio backlog. But you need not overload the portfolio backlog simply by introducing too many products that you will be taking care of in the same time frame.

Many businesses conduct their respective strategic planning events on an annual basis that usually occurs by the 3rd quarter of each fiscal year. One of the results of this type of strategic planning is the production of a product list that they are going to work on for the incoming year. These products are usually placed along with their respective portfolios, which will ultimately overwhelm the planning process of the portfolio.

This does not mean that all organizations need not do any kind of strategic planning. Instead, organizations are supposed to define what their strategic vision is, but they do not have to identify the details that they are going to need to look after to form the strategy. By deciding about the product portfolio, they violate the rule of the use of economically sensible batch sizes.

It is very expensive and wasteful to process a big group of products and then determine how they must be sequenced on portfolio backlog because a large number of products may further complicate the scheduling process. It is a lot simpler to find out the sequence of portfolio backlog if you have a handful of items to manage everything.

You may opt to introduce brand new products to the portfolio at different intervals to prevent the overwhelming of the product backlog. When you find out that you have many more instances for introducing new products, you can effectively cut down on the cost and the effort you have to exhaust to review and insert the products in the portfolio. This makes the planning phase a lot more predictable and stable as well.

When the product backlog size starts growing, you may start to throttle the flow of the product. In order to do this, you may tweak economic filters for improving the product approval standards in a way that only extremely high-quality products may be allowed to get through. This will cut down the tendency of new and random products from entering and establishing a better balance with the departure rate of a product.

When you are planning product portfolios, you must embrace any type of emergent opportunities or the opportunities that are yet unknown to an organization or are unlikely to happen in the organization. Suppose your organization tends to thrive in the online betting marketplace. In that case, you may know that your business is going to operate in a particular environment that is extremely regulated by certain jurisdictions and regulations. You should keep in mind that regulations may be unpredictable, and they highly depend on the policies of the government when we talk about a casino as an organization. If the regulations have to change, you must embrace new opportunities that will pop up suddenly.

Suppose you witness any unexpected change in the environment of an organization, and it is likely to affect the profit or effort that the teams need to spend for certain items in the backlogs. In that case, you must make appropriate insertions and the right releases in portfolio backlogs. Your immediate action will create a productive working environment and help you stay ahead of your competition who may not take appropriate action regarding the right number of opportunities. Let's say you believe in a frequent schedule for the evaluation of opportunities like monthly meetings, and you also have economic filters to work it. You may not feel the need to spend a lot of time on emergent opportunities.

There are many economic benefits that an organization may enjoy, whether it opts for frequent smaller releases. The single most important benefit is that it will elevate their profits. It will also aid them in the prevention of the portfolio from encountering any kind of convoy effect.

Let us first define the convoy effect. It is a phenomenon that is similar to having to drive behind a big and slow-moving vehicle. If you are trapped behind that vehicle, there is a chance that all the drivers who are driving smaller vehicles like you are will feel the same effect. They will feel trapped. When you allow a big number of products in your product backlog, you will create a queue of many small products. As all products will be delayed because of one larger product, the smaller products will start accruing considerable delay costs over the course of time. This will make your profits suffer in the end.

Outflow Strategy Creation

When you have to develop better management that will ultimately help you when you have to pull out all the products from the portfolio backlog, you may use the following strategies.

The first is paying proper attention to the idle work. All the traditional organizations release products into the production phase by taking the following steps. The first step is selecting a product from the portfolio backlog and then assigning it to the people who will deal with it during the development stage. The second step is finding out if everyone is not giving his or her 100 %, you need to repeat the first step.

This particular approach is designed to keep everyone in your organization busy. It does not mean that people will work in a fast and error-free environment on a specific product. Instead of following this risky method, you may aim to work on a specific product when you are pretty sure that the item on your portfolio backlog will not cause any kind of disruption in the workflow that has been started.

Limiting WIP

In the previous chapters, you have already read that it is quite wise to get work from the product backlog when you are pretty sure that the team has developed the capacity to work on it. The same is true for the portfolio backlog.

Knowing the total number of Scrum teams available and what product types they have to handle will aid you in procuring the information you need to know. This includes knowing the number of products your feature teams may easily accommodate on the individual backlogs without spreading to the breaking point to meet their deadlines.

A couple of people who are freed from their tasks does not mean that you must delegate tasks the right way. If you plan to pick a product from the portfolio backlog, you must see that you have got a full team committed to working with a new set of guidelines on a new set of tasks. Even if you have got a bunch of developers who are willing to work on the new product, they should not be the only ones to work on the product. By making them initiate making progress that demands a full team to work on doubles up the miscommunication risk. It will only slow down the work.

In-Process Items

If you have successfully developed the right strategy that deals with the in-process products, it will provide you with guidance on whether you will need to preserve, deliver, or revise a particular product that teams have been working on. You will also know whether to terminate that or not. You should make it a regular practice to make these decisions in a regular way in every sprint. You can also opt for making the decisions during the off-cycle periods when you start receiving unexpected results of certain products that are going to be worked on.

The use of marginal economics is the key strategy that you may use for guidance in the process of decision-making. You also can use it to stay aligned with the core principle of Scrum. The use of marginal economics will help you make decisions about the items that are in progress as per the ROI they are going to generate for the client. Since you are deliberating about profits and return on investment, you have to make a decision whether you will be able to afford the spending of extra resources on the continuous development of the products.

The in-process products may be dealt with the following strategies.

a. The first strategy is preservation. It focuses on continuing with product development. You need to take this particular option when a product justifies all the resources it has already consumed, and you also know that if you continue the development of the product, you will receive a better return on investment (ROI).

b. The second strategy is delivery. It focuses on ceasing the development phase of a product and delivering it right away. You may choose this option if the product has got the minimum releasable features that will be valuable for the end-user and that will also bring about a fair amount of Return on Investment (ROI) for you, without needing any additional investment.

c. The third strategy is about the change of directions as per the new data that you have harvested. This option is viable only when your investment is the least justified, and the product does not have any releasable features. However, you have got an alternate path that you can use to ensure the product's success.

d. The fourth strategy is termination. It is about ceasing the development and killing the product immediately. You have this option if the resources you spend on them are the least justifiable. The product carries no foreseeable value for the end-user, and you lack any logical idea to make the product work.

Many subjective and foolish behaviors may prevent you from making the right decisions for the products you have invested your time and resources in. For example, many people will not take the daring step of terminating a project that has consumed too many resources that is still far from creating a clear picture of how it will work or what value it will produce for the end-user or the owner of the product. Some do not think about terminating the project on which they have spent their first dollar.

Accounting systems have to tolerate these risky assumptions. A company developing software they thought would deliver 100% value to the end-user and the customer may cost about $100,000 to develop fully. After you have spent half the amount on the development, you find out that the product will provide only 15% value to the customers and it will cost $500,000 to develop. Despite the mega difference in the cost, some will keep pursuing the development even after knowing the fact that the value is significant and even ridiculously lower than they would have expected and that the cost cannot be justified. This is not sensible at all.

What Products to Produce?

Before you kick off a sprint and enter the development stage for any product, you must know that you should have a product backlog. You can generate a product backlog by producing a product vision in the first place. You will not know what to accomplish if you have not done the right amount of envisioning about what you need to create.

When you are envisioning a product by using Scrum, you are doing any kind of ceremonial chartering of the project. You do not believe that you can know everything you need to do that. You may need to have a sufficient amount of confidence to ponder upon portfolio planning and decide whether it is appropriate to fund the next level of development or not.

When you arrive at this point, you realize that you can understand you cannot fund the next stage without setting the vision for the product. In order to have a clear mindset on funding the next stage of development, you must understand the features, high-quality solutions, costs, and customers. You may not want to spend time and effort on guesswork and overthinking. You may feel a powerful urge to jump toward sprints where you can have clear feedback on the development stages and where you know whether your solutions will work or not.

Envisioning is a continuous process. You do not just envision the product at the start. You have to keep doing that even after you have gone past the initial stages toward the development stages. You have to pass on the initial idea through the strategic filters of the organization's strategies. That probably is the time when people will investigate as to why the product is worth investment. At this point, you may realize how much ROI you may get from the product and whether the product is worth investing in, in the first place or not.

Conclusion

Now that you have completed the Scrum book, the next step is to put the concepts into practice. Scrum is highly beneficial to speed up processes in industries. It works especially well in the IT industry, where everything has to be highly efficient. From the development of the software to launching it for the end-user, everything needs to speed up, or it will be tangled up in a never-ending loop.

Scrum ensures that all the processes are up to mark, right from the envisioning phase to budget allocation and to the development of the actual product. You will be able to master the Scrum method after you have put it into practice more than once. And once you've done so, you'll be able to sit back and reap the rewards!

References

Project manager responsibilities in Scrum - a realistic view. (n.d.).
Agile Project Management Software -
VivifyScrum. https://www.vivifyscrum.com/insights/project
-manager-responsibilities-in-scrum-a-realistic-view

Redefining the project manager role in Scrum. (n.d.).
AgileConnection. https://www.agileconnection.com/article/r
edefining-project-manager-role-scrum

Scrum development team - Who's in it? | Roles & responsibilities.
(2019, January 3). Professional Certification Courses,
Classroom And Virtual
Trainings. https://www.knowledgehut.com/tutorials/scrum-
tutorial/development-team

Scrum master roles and responsibilities - A deep dive. (2019,
January 3). Professional Certification Courses, Classroom
And Virtual
Trainings. https://www.knowledgehut.com/tutorials/scrum-
tutorial/scrum-master

Scrum master vs product owner: What's the difference? (2021, February 22). Product Manager HQ. https://productmanagerhq.com/scrum-master-vs-product-owner/

What are the 12 Agile principles? | Definition and overview. (2020, July 29). Product Roadmap Software | ProductPlan. https://www.productplan.com/glossary/agile-principles/

What is product backlog in Scrum? Who responsible for it? (n.d.). Ideal Modeling & Diagramming Tool for Agile Team Collaboration. https://www.visual-paradigm.com/scrum/what-is-product-backlog-in-scrum/

www.ingramcontent.com/pod-product-compliance
Lightning Source LLC
Chambersburg PA
CBHW060238030426
42335CB00014B/1514